Chopin's Heart

The Quest to Identify the Mysterious Illness of the World's Most Beloved Composer

Steven Lagerberg

Front Cover Photograph: Jupiterimages/Getty Images

ISBN: 145640296X
ISBN-13: 9781456402969
LCCN: 2010917784

*"Never say you know the last word
about any human heart."*
Henry James

Portrait of Chopin by T. Kwiatkowski.

Contents

Prologue

"A light heart lives long."
William Shakespeare

Stand in front of any small group of adults for more than a few minutes and ask them to describe the things that possess the greatest meaning in their lives and, nearly invariably, although with varying hesitancy, they will at some moment begin to signal with their hands at the center of their chests. Whether with a clenched fist over the breastbone or an opened palm with splayed fingers spread widely across the upper thorax, they will employ a nearly universal human gesture as they passionately disclose the source of their innermost feelings, their concealed wellspring of truth. Science be damned, the heart continues to enjoy its time-tested yet outsized role of being the center of a person's spirit, personality, and character. Throughout recorded history, in literature, music, art, as well as in everyday conversation, the position of the heart as a personification of the human soul remains sacrosanct. Metaphorically bound to our soul, a heart can soften or harden, be open or closed, broken or crushed, but can it also reveal secrets from our past?

Now an extraordinary recent controversy may blur the distinction between the cerebral facts of science and the sentimental fancy of the heart as the seat of the soul. The fateful concurrence of the present scientific search for the identity of the illness that befell the beloved Polish composer, Frédéric Chopin, with the actual existence of his long-preserved heart, now allows Science to partner with Art to tell a story of intrigue and mystery. It is the untold story of Chopin's heart.

What is it about our heart that engenders our deepest feelings? Certainly, it is the magical pump lying deep within our central core, the source of that rhythmic drumming of our soul. Most decidedly, we have come to understand our very lives vitally depend upon its every beat. From ancient times musicians and poets have used that incessant throb to power their ballads and to soothe and stir the spirits of numberless billions. No different from these ancient bards was Chopin, as his distinctly syncopated Slavic rhythms first enchanted his audiences with their originality and daring. Knowing now that Chopin's own rhythmic dynamo may have suffered from some chronic disorder somehow makes that dreadful alliance disturbingly unsettling. Fortunately, for Chopin and for most of us, our heart automatically performs its relentlessly repetitive task, and we remain largely oblivious to its hidden struggles. Our heart's private perseverance, however, may not be the only endowment we take for granted.

Most of us enter adulthood blithely accepting that our quest for our life's aspirations might be accomplished without the threat of a chronic illness. However, not everyone enjoys such good fortune, and reality can sometimes be harsh. Those who manage to achieve their goals despite some disability deserve our profound respect and admiration. Those who cannot, merit our sympathy and understanding. Today's health care advances have allowed countless numbers of those afflicted with chronic health problems to succeed in ways never thought possible only a few decades ago. Far less certain was that success for someone born two hundred years ago. Chopin has long been considered to have suffered from the life-draining disease of tuberculosis. He was ill for more than half his life, seriously so for at least a decade. That he was able to achieve an impressive level of success among those in the highest levels of musical appreciation while battling his disease is truly remarkable. He suffered from a chronic respiratory ailment beginning in his mid-teen years, which extended in a relentlessly progressive and repeating pattern until his eventual death from respiratory insufficiency and heart failure at the age of thirty-nine. The nature of that illness was its chronicity, its decades-long course periodically punctuated by episodes of profound weakness. These weak spells were usually accompanied by incessant coughing and the frightening harbinger of pulmonary hemorrhaging.

Chopin's many biographers have, without exception, concluded that his illness was tuberculosis, ignoring the doubts as to the accuracy of that diagnosis expressed even by some of his own physicians. In more recent years, several medical analyses have suggested alternative possibilities, including, among others, cystic fibrosis, valvular heart disease, a fairly prevalent genetic type of chronic lung disease, and an immunodeficiency disorder.[1,2,3,4,5] Our modern understanding of medical pathology now allows for a wider field of possible diagnostic entities to be included in any intensive analysis of his illness, and so becomes the necessary catalyst for any current review.

Why dwell on the morbid aspects of Chopin's existence rather than the brilliant jewels of his musical output? Isn't his struggle with illness secondary to any concern we have for his legacy? I agree completely with the idea that an analysis can be done of his life's musical achievements without detailing any of his personal struggles with illness. There is a sufficient wealth of material and depth of musicianship in his works to keep any musicologist occupied for a long time.[6] However, I also believe that a more complete understanding of his long ordeal with illness and the personal details of his existence allow the listener to possess a more penetrating insight into Chopin's complex music. In my opinion, the effect Chopin's chronic illness had upon the character of his works has not been adequately explored. The quest to identify the intriguing puzzle of his illness and how it changed his life is an interesting one. Mysteries beg to be solved.

My aim is not to be dogmatic in my hypothesis. My goal is to shed light on this interesting subject. As a physician with an enduring passion for Chopin's works and a keen interest in the intriguing details of his life and illness, I have tirelessly sorted through the existing historical materials searching for the medical clues that might identify his chronic affliction. My collaboration with the superb Polish scientists prepared to undertake the analysis of Chopin's heart and with their indomitable leader, Professor Wojciech Cichy, and my witnessing their resolute plan to unravel its secret mysteries have allowed me exclusive access to the many fascinating and thus far unplumbed details of this historic inquiry.

My passion is to explain, clarify, and encourage a broader interpretation of the known facts, and to invite those scholars interested in historical accuracy to look anew at the available evidence in light of current medical knowledge. I realize any diagnostic certainty will probably be elusive. Without a scientific analysis based on an actual review of tissue samples that someday might be methodologically obtained from the deceased composer's remains, an uncontested final conclusion may be impossible to secure. Such an extraordinarily delicate undertaking is a daunting task, considering all the political, ethical, religious, and practical difficulties this form of investigation would entail. Nevertheless, I favor such a careful scientific inquiry only if authorized by the world's principal Chopin organizations and only if performed by a team of internationally recognized forensic experts. I harbor the fervent hope such an analysis would only increase our respect, understanding, and admiration for this unique individual and encourage those with similar disabilities to keep their aim high in their personal pursuits of life's dreams. What follows is my sincere attempt to tell an interesting story and prepare for that investigation.

"For Where Your Treasure Is, There Your Heart Will Be"

*"Every great achievement is
the victory of a flaming heart."*
Ralph Waldo Emerson

Inside a mighty column behind an ornate marble plaque in Warsaw's Church of the Holy Cross rests the most revered relic in Poland. It is the heart of Frédéric Chopin. The letters carefully carved in the light gray stone spell out the biblical phrase from Luke 12:34, "For where your treasure is, there your heart will be." Preserved in alcohol, some say the finest French cognac, this last-surviving vestige of the beloved composer's remains, two hundred years since its first rhythmic quiver, continues to lure thousands of adoring visitors from every corner of the world. No strangers to the intense passions of Chopin's incomparable music, its joys as well as its inconsolable melancholy, these ardent disciples make their pilgrimages to this far away Baroque cathedral with the fervent hope of capturing some essence of the man himself. It's as if their intimacy with Chopin's actual heart might suddenly cast off the scales from their eyes and lift the veil of mystery shrouding Chopin's genius. How could this mere mortal have written music of such breathtaking grandeur, works with an almost perfect fusion of introspective lyricism and dramatic complexity? How could this sickly man whose life was altogether too brief have gained such a piercing understanding of the human soul and then have been so

1

capable of translating that pathos into music? His flower-strewn sepulcher is an eerily spectral place and, rather inexplicably, many turn away from it with a shiver, filled not only with a greater sense of communion with this extraordinary composer but also an irresistible desire to know more about him. I know. I too was smitten with those passions as I stood before it a decade ago.

The crypt containing Chopin's heart in the Holy Cross Church.

I first encountered this spirit-stirring shrine while attending the 2000 International Chopin Piano Competition. I remember immediately being struck by the intriguing oddity that while Chopin's body lay buried beneath a beautifully sculpted angel in the Père Lachaise cemetery in Paris, here was his heart, entombed in a Polish church nearly a thousand miles away. Why had his heart been separated from his body? Why weren't all of his remains buried in Warsaw at his family's beloved parish church, a mere stone's throw away from where he grew up as a musically precocious child? At the time, I incorrectly surmised the presence of contentious competition for burial rights among his relatives in France and Poland to explain this bizarre discontinuity. I never could have guessed the real reason.

As a physician, I am used to observing people, whether alive or dead, usually in one piece and certainly in one place. Aside from a few scattered saints, few of us wind up having our parts widely strewn about the globe. To me, something seemed missing, and it wasn't just Chopin's body. I immediately suspected there was an interesting story behind Chopin's partitioned parts and was determined to get to the bottom of it—to the heart of the matter, as I joked to myself. Little did I know then that the tale of his heart would only continue to elicit my enduring curiosity for years to come. Eventually I was to learn that the complete story of Chopin's heart remains an untold mystery. Will its labyrinthine secrets ever be revealed?

As he lay slowly dying in his elegant Paris apartment in the Place Vendôme, inexorably losing his abilities to speak and even to breathe, Chopin became terrified about the possibility of being buried alive. Chronically ill for much of his life, he possessed an intimate knowledge of his physical incapacities and must have greatly feared his breathlessness might be mistaken for his death. Perhaps he recalled the tubercular Lord Byron's similar fears and the poet's passionate insistence that his heart be removed upon his demise. More likely, he remembered his own father's deathbed request, a hastily penciled note to his physician, essentially echoing Byron's command, "If this cough suffocates me, I beseech you to have my body opened so that I'll not be buried alive."

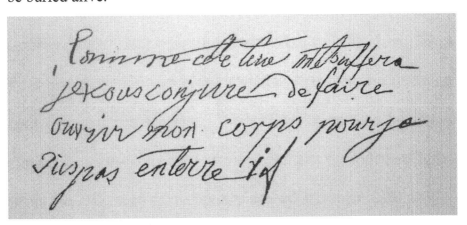

"If this cough should suffocate me, I beseech you to have my body opened that I not be buried alive."

I would come to understand that Chopin's many biographers had for years erroneously ascribed these words to the composer himself, thereby adding a starkly dramatic twist to an already tragic tale. At the time, not particularly concerned with who said what, I found it sadly ironic that both father and son, in the waning moments of their lives, had experienced such a similar terror at the prospect of being buried alive. Personally, the thrust of "like father, like son," penetrated too deeply.

In the hours immediately preceding his death and just as he became aware of his faltering ability to speak, Chopin had hoarsely whispered to his eldest sister, Ludwika, carefully instructing her to have his heart removed after his death and placed in a glass urn. He desperately wished to elude his dreaded fate of suffocation and at the same time extract the promise from his sister that she would return this essence of his "soul" to his beloved Poland. Faithfully adhering to his famous patient's rather ghoulish request, Chopin's last physician, Dr. Jean Cruveilhier, would later remove the dead composer's heart and place it in a crystal vessel filled with alcohol. As his final service to Chopin and his family, he would privately present it to Ludwika. In turn, she would surreptitiously smuggle this cherished core of her brother's body, carefully concealed beneath the layers of her multi-pleated dress, past the menacing stares of the sullen border guards into Russian-occupied Poland, where the relic would eventually find its way to its current resting place, enshrined in Warsaw's historic church.

Later I would learn much more about Chopin's heart, collecting many fascinating details that led to a more complete understanding of the perplexing illness that plagued the Polish genius. I would also eventually unearth a strange twist to this narrative, an unusual story from a most unexpected source. I would be surprised to discover that Chopin's heart had been stealthily removed from its marbled sanctuary during World War II and fortuitously saved from its near-certain destruction during the Polish Uprising of 1944. Even more astonishing, however, was the fascinating story of its last-minute rescue, not by some impassioned Pole, but rather by the foresight of a little-known Nazi chaplain in the occupying German army! How many are now aware that the Nazis used Chopin's preserved heart, nearly one hundred years after its hurried removal from his corpse, as one of their preeminent propaganda tools? Obviously, the Germans realized that with this honored symbol of the Polish spirit in their hands they had a weapon akin to kryptonite in its potency to quell any glimmer of optimism among those in the rapidly emerging Polish resistance movement. I considered it an intriguing phenomenon that not only had Chopin's wondrous works changed the course of music, but that a century later his actual heart, as a beloved assimilation of Poland's soul, had been used in an attempt to sway the course of human history. That one man's heart could accomplish all this was for me quite a revelation.

As luck would have it, the German chaplain's efforts were not in vain. The severe damage to the Holy Cross Church inflicted during the ensuing struggle destroyed its façade, brought down its towers, and cracked the very column where the heart had been interred. As I later became increasingly consumed by the controversy surrounding the identity of the mysterious disease that took away the life of this famous composer, I would often reflect back on this curious episode in the long history of Chopin's heart and wonder if the good chaplain's opportune efforts in rescuing the cherished organ might also have saved it from another accident of history—its misdiagnosis!

In the summer of 2008, I would see a news flash about a Polish investigative team's request to retrieve Chopin's heart once again, this time in order to begin DNA testing in a remarkably bold attempt at diagnosing the illness that felled the famous composer. From Professor Wojciech Cichy, the distinguished leader of that team, I would eventually get to see some of the revealing observations of the heart as recorded sixty-five years earlier by a rather prolific Polish musicologist, Bronisław Edward Sydow. Could these impressions written long ago by a non-scientist be at all helpful in ascertaining the cause of Chopin's illness? I was to find out.

Like a jilted victim in a love triangle, Chopin's heart would soon become the center of a storm of intrigue and controversy. Once again I found myself wishing to know more. Fortunately, I would; yet, before I can relate the complete story of Chopin's heart, it's necessary for me to go back a few years and explain how I became so caught up in my enthusiasm for Frédéric Chopin and his music.

I have long admired Chopin's music and, to my amazement, for much longer than I ever had imagined. I now believe it may have been the first music I can remember hearing. As a four-year-old clumsily fiddling around with a discarded 45 RPM record player, I distinctly recall playing my favorite little clear red plastic disk over and over and being absolutely mesmerized by what I have only recently come to learn was Arthur Rubenstein's thrilling performance of Chopin's impassioned *Polonaise in A flat*, the great *Op. 53*. That precisely cut diamond of pure inspiration, imbued with hard-charging emotion and triumphant spirit, easily gave me goose bumps at the age of four and still does today. Much later in my life, and after carefully surveying the world of music for those works I most admired, I inadvertently became reacquainted with Chopin's works and quickly became endeared to their sensuously pleasing richness and their intellectually challenging inventiveness. It was only during a particularly impassioned recent performance of this great polonaise that my mind suddenly flashed back to that childhood moment of discovery, flooding my emotions with the aching beauty of that never-to-return time.

For many years, Chopin's music existed for me as a rather private passion, always a source of great solace and inspiration. Eventually, to my profound enjoyment, I would become familiar with most of his works and their varied interpretations, and so when the opportunity to attend the 2000 Chopin Competition in Warsaw presented itself, I really had no reason to refuse.

In Warsaw I had the distinct pleasure of meeting a very pleasant Polish-American woman, Jadwiga Gewert[7], our common love for the music of Frédéric Chopin rendering us immediate and fast friends. I discovered this no-nonsense former attorney to be a virtual treasure trove of information about all things related to Chopin and a tireless advocate for young American pianists. As the Executive Director of the Chopin Foundation of the United States, she supervises a National Chopin Piano Competition, innumerable musical activities in the Miami area, as well as the activities of several branch chapters around the country. Promoting the music of Chopin is her life. It's an obvious passion you immediately sense when you meet her. Unbeknownst to me at the time, Jadwiga was to play an increasingly important role in my life.

The Warsaw competition is one of the world's largest and most prestigious musical affairs and a virtual Mecca for Chopin fans. Although there are dozens of these musical events dedicated to a specific composer scattered around the globe, nowhere aside from Poland can one witness the absolute synthesis of the national soul of a country with that composer's art. The love for Chopin's music runs so deeply here that it can supplant the Polish mother tongue, with certain works essentially acting as code words for patriotism, duty, nostalgia, and pride. As with the dramatic opening chords of Beethoven's Fifth Symphony coming to symbolize for many the bold and brave actions of humankind, Chopin's music has in its own unique way played an important role in history. Encrypted messages associated with Chopin's music were used successfully by the Poles in their determined resistance to the German invasion of World War II, when radio broadcasts of his well-known works carried their concealed communications of hope and inspiration to countless thousands of battle-weary citizens. How many lives were saved or soothed by these secret signals transmitted via the wondrous melodies of Chopin's genius will never be known.

Although I always understood that Chopin's music was very popular, at least among classical music enthusiasts, I had never before witnessed the absolute adoration of his works by so many, all crammed together into the impressive Philharmonic Hall in Warsaw. Experiencing this tremendous crowd response must be similar to being swept up in some revolutionary movement or to being overwhelmed by the hysterical ecstasy surging through a feverish mass of humanity at a pounding rock concert. The emotional response I observed at the piano competition in Warsaw was absolutely beyond any of my many previous experiences at predictably sedate classical music concerts. It is in front of such an emotionally charged and passionate constituency that, every five years, the competition's jury struggles with the Herculean task of selecting the most gifted performers from hundreds of talented young pianists. Interestingly, the crowd probably performs the role of the competition's most important adjudicator, its dramatic responses closing the curtain on some hapless performers and likely determining the jury's final verdict in any close decision.

Following my heart-stopping trip to Poland and with my passions still riding high, I returned to Seattle and, with Jadwiga's capable long-distance assistance from Miami, founded and for several years ran a successful Northwest chapter of the Chopin Foundation. That experience only deepened my knowledge and appreciation for Chopin's music and led to my keen interest in discovering more of the details about his life. The mystery of his heart, however, stuck with me. With my extensive medical background, determining the exact cause of Chopin's illness and investigating the telltale clues to its identity remained a source of intense curiosity for me. Chopin's many fine biographers had all steadfastly maintained that the Polish composer suffered from the ravages of tuberculosis and that this ancient scourge was the cause of his early death at the age of thirty-nine. There appeared to be no debate on this matter but, with my ingrained medical training forcing me to explore this unquestioned assumption, I remained far from certain. I felt the historical evidence did not consistently support the tuberculosis theory, yet I was unable to disprove it with any factual evidence. Like a secret diary locked away in a dusty attic trunk, my lingering doubt would long remain only my own private conjecture.

As I retired from my busy medical practice I eagerly anticipated leaving the confining cubicles of my busy exam rooms and having the freedom to investigate the intriguing mystery about Chopin at my leisure. Medicine may have been my chosen career but, while it still remains a subject of my continued fascination and interest, my consuming pastimes now have evolved into the appreciation of art and music. Specifically, scrutinizing the music of Chopin and uncovering the details of his life continue to be my favorite interests. All this became suddenly easier as my wife and I decided to spend a good part of the year living at our apartment in Paris.

I had come to love Paris for its physical beauty, its deep admiration for the arts, its rich and complex history, not to mention its strong and enduring connection with Chopin. He spent half of his tragically abbreviated life in Paris, quickly establishing his fame and carefully crafting the many beautiful works that continue to astonish musical audiences today. It was the city where he found his greatest success, where his musical genius could be fully appreciated, and where he eventually would sicken and die. I've concluded that rediscovering Chopin's legacy in Paris can be an everyday occurrence, as Paris competes only with Warsaw for the number of daily concerts featuring his music. Audiences and artists alike never seem to tire of it. Although Paris is a delightful challenge all by itself and one of my favorite places, I had been eager to explore more of France. That wish was to be fulfilled by an unexpected request.

The first warm days of spring 2008 had just arrived in France. After enduring the long and sometimes bitterly cold winter weather Paris is known for, I had prepared a long list of interesting things I wanted to do. So when Jadwiga asked me to drop everything and attend a meeting that next week of the International Federation of Chopin Societies[8] in Nohant, France, I was a little unsure how to respond. Initially, I wasn't prepared to go.

Undoubtedly, Jadwiga was aware my obsession with Chopin was the ace up her sleeve and, as she had so presciently anticipated, I needed little persuasion to go. What I had read about Nohant in the numerous biographies of Chopin indicated it was the site of an ancestral home highly cherished by George Sand, Chopin's fascinating companion for some nine years. It was also the place Chopin had spent many lovely summers, far from the oppressive heat of Paris, and where he was able to compose, freed from the constraints of his hectic teaching schedule. Nohant also became the private hermitage where he would ask many of his dearest friends to join him, his most favored being the French Romantic painter, Eugène Delacroix. I was excited to have the opportunity to venture beyond the confines of Paris and to visit a historically significant place in the life of my favorite composer. I felt going to Nohant could be a grand adventure. Luckily, it turned out to be just that.

Nohant is a tiny hamlet in north-central France, a couple of hours from Paris by train and car. It sits atop one of the many gently rolling hills in a vast pastoral farmland, its verdant heights speckled here and there with the occasional ancient limestone chateau. So small one can drive through it in less than a minute, Nohant's only claim to fame rests with the fact that it was the home of that prolific and celebrated French novelist with a man's name, George Sand. She was Aurore Baronne Dudevant (born Dupin) and had appropriated that odd pseudonym in 1832 during her stormy relationship with a manic-depressive and consumptive young law student, Jules Sandeau. She had recently completed a new novel, *Indiana*, and in the custom of the time desired to use a man's name as its author. As the day she embraced this notion was St. George's Day, she paired "George" with a contraction of Sandeau to immortalize her newly formed romantic bond with her young lover.[9] From that time on, Aurore used this new name on all occasions, professional and personal. Interestingly, Chopin in his broken French always called her "Aurora," never acceding to her wish for the appellation George. His refined sensibility would not allow for it, I suspect. Sand would soon establish herself as an extraordinarily popular writer of novels and political discourse who would succeed wildly in a man's world, but not before she would become the cross-dressing, cigar-smoking, fateful companion of Frédéric Chopin.

Together for nearly a decade, these two oddly paired individuals, the increasingly frail composer and the strong-willed Sand, spent their summers at the idyllic country estate in Nohant, far removed from the crowded city of their fame. Those quiet pastoral summers proved to be a fruitful time for Chopin, where, relieved from his constant teaching responsibilities, his dread of the noxious air, and the constant contagion of the city, he was able to compose many of his most beautiful works, including the astounding *Ballade in F minor*, the charming *Berceuse*, and the lovely *Barcarolle*. Without Nohant, both Chopin's life and his legacy would have been remarkably different.

As I was preparing to leave Paris for Nohant, I had spotted a brief headline on the Web about Chopin that piqued my interest and prompted innumerable questions. It also brought back my memories of that moment I stood in front of his heart's shrine in Warsaw. A small article in *The Times of India* reported that a Polish investigative team, led by the leading Polish cystic fibrosis expert, Professor Wojciech Cichy, claimed that cystic fibrosis, and not tuberculosis, had been the illness most likely suffered by Chopin, and that this group was preparing a full-scale inquiry.[10] Cichy stated, "From early childhood he was weak, prone to chest infections, wheezing, coughing." He went on, "If we can prove Chopin suffered from cystic fibrosis, it would be a huge inspiration for our patients, especially children, to know they can accomplish a great deal like he did." Not only did this team announce plans to unseal the crystal urn containing the composer's heart, that near-sacred relic securely entombed in the Holy Cross Church, but they also proposed plans to unearth the remains of Chopin's younger sister, Emilia, who had died suddenly and quite dramatically at the age of fourteen from complications of a chronic illness considered at the time to be tuberculosis. As I digested this news, I imagined Chopin's heart hurriedly thumping away in dreaded anticipation, lying deep in its dark sepulchral prison. This was shocking information for me, disturbing as well as exciting. I was eager to find out if someone at the conference knew more about this. I was not to be disappointed.

I arrived in Nohant not knowing a soul, yet determined to examine its past and probe its gathered experts for answers to some questions I only recently had formulated. Through my past reading about Chopin, I had reluctantly agreed with his biographers, begrudgingly accepting the common opinion that pulmonary tuberculosis was the most likely cause of Chopin's illness and eventual death before the age of forty. I had acquiesced to this opinion solely for a lack of a better explanation. Nevertheless, my medical training always urged me to reject all presumptions made without demonstrative scientific proof and compelled me to harbor a degree of doubt. There were inconsistencies in the historical record that had raised nagging concerns in my mind as to the accuracy of the tuberculosis theory.

Nohant, the ancestral home of George Sand (front view).

Nohant (rear view). The window on the second floor was Chopin's room where he composed and played.

The gardens at Nohant.

Two centuries ago and without any basic understanding of the common illness now known as tuberculosis, how could those ill-equipped and poorly trained physicians have been so sure this was Chopin's disease? That mainstay of tuberculosis diagnosis, the chest x-ray, was not invented until many years later, and even the lowly stethoscope, invented in Paris in 1816 by the French physician, René Laennec, had been introduced in its crudest form by that city's medical practitioners only a few years prior to Chopin's death.[11] Tuberculosis was not even accepted as being an infectious disease until several decades after Chopin's death in 1849, and its varied clinical manifestations continue to confound the best medical practitioners to this day. Without a basic understanding of this illness and without the rudimentary tools of the trade, how could those mid-nineteenth century practitioners have been so certain?

Fortunately, I met many interesting and knowledgeable people in Nohant. Leaders of Chopin organizations from all over the world, they were experts on his music as well his personal history. Grzegorz Michalski, at the time the director of the esteemed Fryderyk Chopin Institute in Warsaw, together with Professor Theodor Kanitzer, the president of the IFCS, conducted the conference and served as its delightful hosts. From them and others I quickly learned about Professor Cichy's bold plans and more about the theory of cystic fibrosis being the leading candidate to replace tuberculosis as Chopin's disease. My medical background gave me an advantage in understanding the differences between these two illnesses and allowed me a respectful appreciation of the methods that would be required for any successful scientific investigation. Armed with that specific knowledge, I could foresee the enormous challenge of such an inquiry and, after considering the often-frustrating current limitations of DNA analysis, I personally doubted it could be accomplished, much less approved, by all the necessary authorities. From what I would come to learn later, my concerns were well founded.

Some years earlier I had been fascinated to read Russell Martin's bestselling book, *Beethoven's Hair*, and to learn that a forensic investigation suggested the famous German composer likely suffered from lead poisoning.[12] Martin astutely theorized that Beethoven acquired this poisonous metal in accumulatively toxic amounts from the various medical potions given him by his physicians in their fruitless efforts to treat his deafness and other ailments. However well intentioned, these lead-laden poultices and pills only served to aggravate the composer's physical state and accentuate the amplitude of his already volatile personality. I found this forensic discovery about the long-dead composer very interesting. The last years of his life must have been a living nightmare for this tortured musical genius, worsened by the very remedies he so eagerly sought to improve his health. Since reading Martin's interesting work, I had seen reports of posthumous medical investigations into the lives of other composers, namely Schubert, Schumann, Paganini, and Ravel, and wondered if a similar inquiry into Chopin's life might also reveal new information sufficient to alter our present understanding of his illness.

There was information just waiting to be discovered. I longed to know more. Soon, I was to begin my search for the mysterious clues that would eventually help provide the answers to my many questions. Would Chopin's long-preserved heart, trapped in its stone pillar in Warsaw, now be able to provide the world with the final clues to its mysterious malady?

Following My Heart

*"Few are those who see with their own
eyes and feel with their own hearts."*
Albert Einstein

Ever since his death in 1849, popular interest in the life of Chopin
and his works has remained uninterruptedly strong. His highly
esteemed reputation appears now to be growing and seems nearly
indestructible as more and more listeners become captivated by his
legendary life story and the distinctive originality and beauty of his
exceptional music. Few composers, even the great J. S. Bach, have
enjoyed such remarkably persistent renown. This popularity, however
well deserved, owes much of its success to the carefully crafted image
of Chopin as the archetypal composer of the Romantic Age, a portray-
al arising from the many first-hand apocryphal accounts of his persona
and performances published during his lifetime and also imaginatively
depicted in his first biography, written by Franz Liszt in 1852.[13] The
glorified representation of the suffering genius of the piano, commu-
nicating emotional sensitivities while passionately inflamed by his
heroic struggle with a morbid illness, has quite dramatically served to
strengthen his legend and guarantee its longevity.

Admittedly, many novel features of Chopin's life only reinforce
that somewhat embellished narrative. His much-publicized affair with
the androgynous female novelist, George Sand, his exile from his
beloved homeland, his meteoric rise to fame after his entry into Paris,
and his early death at the age of thirty-nine all contribute to that rather
tragic image of Chopin now burned indelibly into our imaginations.

What might not be so well known is that Chopin's life was marked more by his struggles with intense inner turmoil than by any action, travel, or adventure. As James Huneker, one of Chopin's early biographers, wrote, "He lived, loved, and died; and not for him were the perils, prizes, and fascinations of a hero's career. He fought his battles within the walls of his soul—we may note and enjoy them in his music."[14] Indeed, listening to Chopin's music more and paying less attention to his legend may be the most informative path to comprehending the man behind the music. Listen to his polonaises, especially the *Polonaise in F sharp minor, Op. 44* or his *Polonaise in A flat, Op. 53*, the latter one burned into my own toddler's embryonic memory, to get an idea of his intense patriotism. Listen to his mazurkas, beginning with the friskiness of the *D major, Op. 33, no. 2* to understand his essential capriciousness. Move on to the elegant sophistication of those of his *Op. 50* and, finally, sample the lushness and inner strength projected by the late mazurkas of *Op. 59*. Turn down the lights, get comfortable, and prepare yourself to savor the depths of nostalgia and melancholy pervading his many nocturnes. What a trip you will have, but during the enchanting journey you will come to know who this man was.

The literature on Chopin is vast and, although today much of it is out of print, it continues to expand and add to our knowledge of both the man and his complex yet easily embraced music. Only fairly recently, however, has there been any objective review of his health problems, a field of inquiry undeniably aided by advances in medical understanding. Over the years, his biographers have accepted his illness as being tuberculosis and have largely ignored other conjectures. After all, there was little reason to dispute the accepted wisdom. Many of Chopin's own physicians, and there were many, labeled him with the presumptive diagnosis of "consumption," or "phthisis," the terms of his era for a complex entity that only many decades later was fully identified as tuberculosis. The reports from those of his physicians who were not quite as certain of his disease were merely passed off as irrelevant inconsistencies and ascribed to the widespread medical ignorance of the times. Besides, the story of the consumptive long-suffering artist was a popular sentiment, one his biographers have not dared to challenge.

During the Romantic Movement, the superstition surrounding the presence of consumption in the artist took on a significance far

Cruveilhier's critically descriptive words written in private correspondence have been salvaged, and these have only served to tantalize the imagination of forensic scholars for years. They certainly attracted my interest.

As a medical student and later as a practicing physician, I was frequently required to "present the case" or, in other words, tell the story of a particular patient's illness to another medical professional. To do it well, one needs to summarize succinctly all of the relevant facts associated with that individual's health problems and present them orally in a relatively brief and comprehensible way. This narrative must unfold in a chronological fashion and without interjecting any subjective impressions along the way, a non-scientific failing most of us are normally prone to do. Over and over, I practiced these skills to the point of proficiency, yet I soon learned that often just how the case was presented would likely determine the conclusions made by the recipients of this information. That is, their opinions were entirely determined by how skillfully the material was arranged and edited. It soon became obvious that a selective manipulation of the facts could persuade the recipients into arriving at a conclusion not necessarily supported by a more objective review of the available information. Facts are facts but, as we all know, they sometimes can be arranged, emphasized, and modified in ways that can result in differing interpretations of the same evidence, leading, rather surprisingly, to quite conflicting conclusions. How a story is told is critical to its understanding. I need to review how the story of Chopin's illness shouldn't be told.

Having sorted through the literature promoting the various theories proposed for Chopin's illness, I believe some well-meaning authors have too often gleaned only what they felt necessary to corroborate their case from the available sources of information about Chopin, at times ignoring other evidence not supportive of their hypothesis. This process of selecting out only those features from a story that support the intended final conclusion of a particular theory often makes for a convincing argument, but it interferes with obtaining the most scientifically accurate appraisal. This stretching of the facts is human nature, I suppose, but it only confounds the successful achievement of a more objective scientific analysis.

Dr. John O'Shea's article, "Was Frédéric Chopin's illness actually cystic fibrosis?" in the December 1987 issue of *The Medical Journal of*

Australia is, I believe, an example of this selective bias.[22] Dr. O'Shea attempts to make a strong case for cystic fibrosis by a discretionary telling of the story. It is a well-known observation that the vast majority of patients with longstanding cystic fibrosis develop a peculiar bulbous enlargement of their fingertips, a condition doctors call clubbing. In finding a way to admitting that it was not at any time recognized in Chopin (even in the plaster casts of the composer's hands taken just after his death), O'Shea counters, "However, Chopin's penchant for wearing gloves is well known," as if wearing gloves could hide this famous man's fingers from the view of so many. His fingers were the lifeblood of his art and any problem with them, however minor, would have been of enormous significance to him and easily spotted by the many others close to him.

To support his premise that Chopin suffered from infertility, another characteristic of males with cystic fibrosis (they may lack the sperm-conducting tube, the vas deferens), O'Shea writes, "Chopin never fathered a child despite his frequent sexual liaisons." He maintains Chopin enjoyed a rather sybaritic lifestyle. Possibly, Dr. O'Shea may have unwittingly acquired his understanding of Chopin's supposedly numerous amorous affairs from what was at that time a very popular rumor. For many years, a belief widely circulated asserting that written evidence had survived to support the notion of Chopin's being sexually profligate. This attestation arose out of what was once claimed to be the composer's own handwritten and often-lurid correspondence with a longtime female acquaintance. Regardless of just how much this information may have influenced Dr. O'Shea and his infertility hypothesis for Chopin, retracing the origins of this supposition about the composer's sexual proficiency is an interesting little story in itself.

In 1945—a very dark time in Polish history—a Polish woman by the name of Czernicka created an international sensation when she produced copies of what she warranted were the long-lost love letters Chopin had written to the attractive and musically talented Polish countess Delfina Potacka. In these impassioned letters, the originals of which had somehow been destroyed, Chopin comes across as a veritable sexual athlete, complete with a sexually based theory to explain his art. He writes quite explicitly about how extraordinarily much he enjoys the pleasures of the flesh with the beautiful countess (and others), yet he bemoans the subsequent loss of his musical creativity with each of his frequent sexual emissions. In an uncharacteristically familiar and earthy writing style, he claims he would obtain immeasurably greater artistic inspiration by adhering to sexual abstinence. Interestingly and rather suspiciously straining the credibility of Madame Czernicka's claims, the psychoanalyst Sigmund Freud had advanced that very same concept in his writings just a few years prior to her "discovery" of these avowedly sultry epistles. This being wartime in Poland, Czernicka's copies were simply received and set aside for later review. It would be several decades before her astonishing claims and letters were all clearly exposed to be an elaborate fakery and a very clever hoax, yet this spurious notoriety and its damage to the common assessment of Chopin's character would persist.

Anyone at all familiar with the life and accurately documented correspondence of Frédéric Chopin must conclude that this complex and sensitive man most assuredly did not engage in frequent sexual encounters. The opposite is more likely. As much as he thoroughly enjoyed the company of his female companions, its liveliness, and its associated social banter, that's about as far as it went. Chopin's lifetime sexual liaisons might safely be counted on one hand. Even George Sand, who spent nearly ten years living with the composer, repeatedly claimed her life with him was nearly completely asexual. Although O'Shea's premise that Chopin was afflicted with cystic fibrosis may someday prove to be correct, he may have based at least some of his suppositions on seriously flawed facts. Evidence based on misinformation is misleading, another demonstration of the well-known principle of garbage in, garbage out.

Unfortunately, there's more. When discussing Chopin's dietary habits, O'Shea writes,[23] "There is considerable evidence to indicate Chopin suffered pancreatic insufficiency, which is associated with cystic fibrosis. The most telling was his extreme emaciation. Careful study of his dietary habits shows he had a preference for a high carbohydrate diet, and avoided fatty foods assiduously. We know he subsisted on bread and confectionery which were supplemented with lean fish or chicken; this was not the staple diet of the people of northern Europe. When Chopin lost a great deal of weight after a respiratory illness at 15 years of age, his doctor found that a high carbohydrate diet enabled Chopin to regain weight...Chopin developed a polyphagia [a big appetite] for carbohydrates."

While fastidious in his habits and fussy about his food, Chopin was most certainly thin, yet he wasn't emaciated during most of his life and lived and dined quite comfortably. The story of Chopin is not another tale of the starving artist. The high-carbohydrate diet recommended by his childhood physician was simply common sense. As an example of an account at odds with this claim of marked dietary deprivation is an observation reported by Józef Brzowski, a Polish musician who spent several years in Paris and who recorded in his diary an account of a lavish dinner Chopin had hosted for him and his good friend, Jan Matuszyński, at the well-known restaurant Au Rocher de Canal in Paris. Brzowski wrote, "Chopin had reserved a private dining room upstairs in the restaurant and, after consulting the menu ordered the meal for all of them. They started with oysters, then had soup, venison, fish cooked in wine sauce, and fresh asparagus."[24] They finished their meal with desserts and champagne. Chopin was also known to love his daily hot chocolate made with generous portions of fresh cream. Dr. O'Shea appears to have arrived at his conclusions too quickly and can be criticized for making some rather sweeping generalizations. There are assumptions and conclusions made in his paper that are not well supported by the historical record. The author has played loose with some facts and has exaggerated others to suit his purpose. In this, he does the study of Chopin's illness a disservice.

In 1995, only a few years following the publication of O'Shea's thought-provoking article, a French researcher, Dr. Jean-Claude Davila, presented a detailed study of Chopin's illness to the faculty at the Paul-Sabatier Medical School in Toulouse, France.[25] In his careful analysis, a study that painstakingly sorted through all of Chopin's correspondence for any clues to the identity of his disease, Dr. Davila came to just the opposite conclusion.

While acknowledging that Chopin's chronic intestinal and respiratory problems might plausibly lead some to consider cystic fibrosis for the Polish composer's illness, Dr. Davila rather quickly dismissed that diagnostic theory as being fundamentally impossible. He could not accept that anyone with cystic fibrosis, especially an individual living in the early part of the nineteenth century, deprived of even the most elementary necessities of care could possibly have survived for nearly four decades! Not accepting O'Shea's cystic fibrosis hypothesis and unable to unearth any other satisfactory alternatives, this French researcher retreated and returned to tuberculosis as being the most certain cause of Chopin's illness and death. The Frenchman couldn't fathom any other reasonable explanation.

Dr. Davila had conducted a careful study, an analysis that vigorously pursued many of the relevant items in the historical record yet, as with Dr. O'Shea's contention, he derived a conclusion from an incomplete knowledge of the facts. What was now needed was for there to be a study possessing greater objectivity and a wider scope of pathologic inquiry, one that could synthesize these differing hypotheses with the latest medical knowledge. As research into cystic fibrosis would begin to advance rapidly at about that same time, medical researchers would come to learn much more.

Reading a far more balanced view can be like taking a breath of fresh air. In their paper, "The Long Suffering of Frédéric Chopin," published in 1998 in *Chest,* the Journal of the American College of Chest Physicians,[25] the authors Kubba and Young rather accurately describe the health issues evident in the history of Chopin and then go on to discuss the many diagnostic possibilities in a straightforward methodological manner. Finally, they present their reasoned analysis and conclude that he suffered either from "a mild form of cystic fibrosis or alpha 1-antitrypsin deficiency," another genetically inherited illness that I will describe later in more detail. Their paper really started the ball rolling for others to delve into this issue and became the model for other studies. However good their paper is at outlining the various possibilities and weighing the evidence, I feel even they fall prey to some exaggeration in an effort to prove their point.

At the age of sixteen, it is clear the young Chopin fell ill with what appeared to be a fairly serious illness. This was really the first reported significant heath problem of Chopin's adolescence, and it needs to be studied carefully for any details it might add to our investigation. As Kubba and Young state, "He had an illness lasting 6 months, in which respiratory complaints, severe headaches, and cervical adenopathy [lymph node swelling in the neck] were prominent symptoms." Indeed, a careful reading of Chopin's correspondence during the time of that illness of early February, 1826, confirms his initial complaints, yet does not support the presumption that those symptoms all lasted six months. A much more likely conclusion can be gleaned from a reading of his correspondence and would support that there was initially an acute phase with those described symptoms lasting for some weeks that was followed by a prolonged period of recovery, during which the young man was quite able to continue his musical studies and interests in relative comfort. What that illness was has not been clearly identified, but it has been compared to mononucleosis or a streptococcal pharyngitis (severe sore throat).

Some believe this illness, suffered during his adolescence, may have been Chopin's initial infection with tuberculosis and may have quite possibly been acquired from his younger sister, Emilia, who herself was ill at the time. It is well recognized that the initial response to the tuberculosis bacterium is usually accompanied by pronounced cervical lymph node swelling (scrofula), fever, fatigue, and respiratory congestion. His family's physician, a Dr. Roemer, considered Chopin to be suffering from some sort of a "catarrhal infection" and duly applied leeches to the boy's neck, then the popular treatment of the times.[26] Chopin's acute illness left him with fatigue and some weight loss that stretched out for months, prompting his concerned parents to send him that next summer, along with Emilia, to the well-known health spa at Reinertz (now Duszniki). Emilia was already chronically ill with her own respiratory complaints. For a long time, she had been suffering from repeated bouts of coughing often accompanied by significant amounts of fresh bleeding, a condition known as *hemoptysis*. Her physicians at the time appeared convinced she was suffering from tuberculosis, a diagnosis few historians have attempted to refute, yet one modern investigators have now challenged.

While at Reinertz, Chopin wrote to a friend in Warsaw, "I have not yet been for the excursions that everybody takes, because it's forbidden to me…near Reinertz there is a mountain…but the air is not good for everybody, and unluckily I am one of those patients to whom it is not allowed."[27] Obviously, the illness, whatever it was, must have significantly reduced his respiratory capacity and made strenuous exercise either uncomfortable or impossible. The diagnostic possibilities at this point are many and include, among others, tuberculosis, mononucleosis, streptococcal pharyngitis with an associated endocarditis (an inflammation in the lining of the heart and its valves), and pneumonia with complications.

Kubba and Young go on to state, "He suffered similar complaints while in Vienna in 1830 (at age twenty)." I am unable to confirm Chopin suffered from any serious illness during his stay in Vienna. While there, his correspondence shows he occupied much of his time attempting to establish his presence in the local musical community, finishing his *Études Op. 10*, giving a few concerts, meeting with the principal local musicians. At the same time he appeared generally overwhelmed by his indecision as to whether he should go on to Paris. There is no record of a similar illness during that interval. In fact, he fortunately managed to evade the local contagion of the season. Chopin's opportune departure from Vienna allowed him to avoid becoming a casualty of the huge cholera epidemic that had originated that same year in India and had later spread through Russia and Poland. This virulent contagion had arrived in Austria only days before the young pianist's travel to Munich and Stuttgart. That he was indecisive as to his career plans and a little lazy there can be little doubt, but to state that he suffered a comparable illness to that of 1826 appears unsupported by the evidence.

O'Shea, Kubba and Young, and others have attempted to tell the story and furnish some valuable clues as to Chopin's illness, albeit often in a sometimes selective manner and with an added emphasis on some points at the expense of others. Clearly, there is controversy over the sometimes confusing details of the historical record. In these and other sources, an accurate depiction of Chopin's physical state is often difficult to ascertain, yet there is a story to tell, a mystery still to be solved. There exist pieces of information gathered from diverse sources that, when combined into an intriguing whole, form an interesting narrative from which reasonable conclusions might be drawn. A comprehensive objective analysis is what is needed and begs to be told, carefully and completely, as the way the story is told is critical to understanding this enigma. Before exploring the details of the medical possibilities any further, it's necessary to stop and review Chopin's life story, pausing along the way to examine and emphasize those items pertaining to his health in greater detail. I need now to keep following my heart in an attempt to tell this story without bias or distortion.

The Early Years

*"Your work is to discover your world and then
with all your heart give yourself to it."*
Buddha, 563-483 BC

Fryderyk Franciszek Chopin[28] was born on March 1, 1810, in Żelazowa Wola, a small village thirty miles west of Warsaw, to a poor Polish woman of noble ancestry and a forty-year-old French instructor who had immigrated to Poland in 1787. Although there still exists some confusion about the exact day of Frédéric's birth, there is no conjecture about the unremarkable span of his infancy, except if you count the several apocryphal stories claiming the infant would start to cry whenever he heard music. He was the third of four children and the only male, ensuring he would be forever fussed over in a house filled with women. Barely six months after his birth, the family moved to nearby Warsaw, where Chopin's father had secured a teaching post at the Saxon Palace, teaching both French and French Literature. The family was not poor, yet not by any means wealthy. By all accounts, it was a happy home.

Żelazowa Wola, Chopin's birthplace.

Although neither parent claimed any special aptitude, they both were musical. Nicholas, Chopin's father, described as a cautious and somewhat phlegmatic fellow, was modestly talented on the flute and violin. Justyna, Chopin's mother, almost mouse-like in her demeanor and yet full of gentleness and warmth, was almost certainly the one with the most enthusiasm for music. Frédéric fondly remembered the frequent music-making in the Chopin home, with his mother often seated at the family piano singing Polish folksongs. Three of the four Chopin children developed strong literary and musical interests, with Emilia, Frédéric's younger sister, becoming perhaps the most artistically gifted of his siblings. Tragically, she would die at the age of fourteen, a victim of a chronic disease thought at the time to be tuberculosis.[29] In their very brief time together, Emilia and Frédéric would share a very special bond, but did they also share the same illness?

Justyna and Nicholas, Chopin's parents.

Frédéric, at the age of four, had become an avid pupil of his mother's informal piano teaching, acquiring the rudiments of the keyboard extraordinarily quickly. By the time he was six, it was obvious he had a very special proficiency in music. He was already showing an amazing gift for improvisation, a skill he loved to demonstrate again and again. Years later, performing in the elegant music salons of Paris and surrounded by the astounded and adoring audiences of the cultural elite, he would continue to entertain himself with this musical facility. Fortunately, Frédéric's attentive parents were quick to note his remarkable accomplishments. Needing to expand Frédéric's instruction beyond their own limited capabilities, they decided to entrust their seven-year-old's continuing musical education to the services of a rather disheveled and toothless Bohemian (Czech) immigrant, the colorful and intelligent violinist, Wojciech (Adalbert) Żywny. According to the family stories, this unusual fellow never bathed, preferring only an occasional rubdown with vodka during spells of hot weather.[30] That this unlikely character became the first instructor for the child who would someday succeed in being one of the finest composers and pianists of the nineteenth century is a story in itself. However, Żywny had a greatly beneficial influence on his young pupil, providing him with the fundamentals of music theory and instilling in him an enduring love for the great classical composers. From Żywny, Chopin acquired his lifelong passion for Bach and Mozart and a thorough understanding of Hummel and Haydn. As his teacher hadn't any formal piano instruction himself, the young Chopin inventively developed his own method of piano playing and mastered it so well that Żywny wisely decided to leave the boy's self-learned skills well enough alone. To his good fortune, Chopin's future music instructor would follow suit, recognizing the boy's prodigious inherent keyboard abilities and daring not to interfere. In this, his teachers were very wise not to stifle Chopin's burgeoning genius.

Adalbert Żywny, Chopin's first music teacher.

Barely a year later, Frédéric had become a local celebrity in Warsaw and was being favorably compared to the young Mozart. Before his eighth birthday, he had already composed works he was to perform to great acclaim at a public concert at the Saxon Palace. The *Warsaw Review* observed, "The composer of this dance, only eight years of age, is a real musical genius…if this boy had been born in Germany or France, his fame would probably by now have spread to all nations."[31] At the age of only eight, Chopin's concert career appeared predestined.

The young Chopin much preferred the joys of playing his piano, writing plays with his sisters, and leading an active social life to the rough-and-tumble antics that captivate so many young boys. His avoidance of competitive athletics may have been ordained by his slender and small frame, or it might have simply been a matter of preference. Most likely it was a little of both. Some medical investigators see his inactivity as a sure sign of a constitutional weakness, even suggestive of a congenital heart defect. Others claim he may have suffered from asthma. However, there does not appear to be sufficient evidence in the historical records to support either of these claims. He apparently enjoyed reasonable health at this time in his life, although one of his youthful acquaintances, Eustachy Marylski, described him as "something of a weakling."[32]

His parents would become increasingly worried about his health and especially his perplexing failure to put on much weight as he grew into adolescence. There have been reports that Chopin later in life suffered from digestive complaints and varied food intolerances, especially to fatty foods. Whether this was actually the case or whether his parents were simply concerned about his diminutive frame cannot be reliably determined by a review of the existing records. His possible digestive difficulties, nevertheless, play an important role in the current debate over the identification of his chronic illness.

One of the proposed illnesses Chopin could have suffered is cystic fibrosis, a disease usually marked by chronic and severe intestinal disturbances. Regardless of the cause of the young Chopin's slight size, his parents were sufficiently concerned about him to seek medical advice. Whenever he was away from home visiting friends, a special dietary regimen recommended by his family doctor went along with him. Essentially, it was a high-calorie diet. By one account, his meals were to be supplemented with linden extract, roasted acorn coffee, a daily dose of pills to promote weight gain, and an exclusive ration of white rolls, baked expressly for him.[33,34] The dark rye peasant bread that Chopin favored, was for some odd reason never allowed. The composition of the pills he took has never been determined, but it's likely they may have been local folk remedies of little consequence. As with parents everywhere, desperation to find any remedy for an ailing child can foster frenzied and rather bizarre attempts for a cure.

By the age of fifteen, the young Chopin's amazing musical skills had advanced to the degree that he was featured in a major concert honoring Tsar Alexander, who was to become the supreme leader during the Russian occupation of Poland. Chopin performed on an odd instrument called an aeolomelodikon and, much to his everlasting delight, he was awarded with a diamond ring by the tsar as a token of the latter's enjoyment of the music and esteem for the boy. It appears that accepting such a gift from a widely feared ruler not exactly cherished by the common populace of Warsaw wasn't an issue for the young artist! As if this concert's success weren't enough, and planned to coincide with the tsars visit, Chopin's *Rondo in C minor, Op. 1* was published that same week. Timing is always everything.

The first recorded significant illness suffered by the young Chopin occurred when he was sixteen, and his prolonged ordeal was detailed in his letter to one of his best childhood friends, Jan Białobłocki. His own words described the situation:

> You may suppose that all this scribbling is being done at a table; you're wrong, it's from under my quilt, and comes out of a head that's tied up in a nightcap because it's been aching, I don't know why, for the last four days. They have put leeches on my throat because the glands have swelled, and our Roemer says it's a catarrhal affection. It's true that from Saturday to Thursday I was out every evening, till 2 in the night; but it's not that, because I always slept it off in the morning. I should bore you if I wrote any more about such an illness to you who are so much more ill, therefore I will fill up the remainder of this paper with something else.[35]

When the young Chopin writes of his worry over boring his friend, he is referring to Białobłocki's own health problem, a painful chronic infection in his leg, for which he was being treated at another health spa. Unfortunately, his good friend would succumb to bone tuberculosis a year later, presumably from an extension or complication of this same leg infection. That Chopin's illness lasted months is attested by his next letter to his friend, written over three months later, in which he states, "I am really ashamed to have been so long in answering your letter; but various circumstances which have steadily pursued me (I think you can understand my condition this year, because you yourself have had to go through it) just didn't allow me to do as I wished to do."

What was this illness? It could have been *mononucleosis*, an infectious viral infection lasting weeks to months with a predilection for young individuals whose health may already be compromised by nutritional or sleep deficiencies. Its clinical characteristics nearly always include a prolonged sore throat, lymph node swelling in the neck (and elsewhere), fatigue, and poor appetite. Nearly two hundred years later, no cure is yet available, with its current treatment regimen mimicking that of the nineteenth century—primarily medical exhortations for rest and adequate nutrition. Fortunately, however, for today's youth, leeches are no longer part of the treatment! Recovery from mononucleosis takes weeks, sometimes months, and while largely the rule, a chronic form does occasionally occur, especially in those whose general heath is poor and whose duration of recuperation is insufficient.

The young Chopin's illness might simply have been a severe cold, but as his symptoms persisted for such a long time, some think it could have been a streptococcal infection of the throat, complicated subsequently by an associated heart problem. This furtive phenomenon is best known as *rheumatic fever*, the inflammatory condition that can sometimes rather silently occur several weeks after a Group A streptococcal infection.[36] It's believed to be caused by a smoldering antibody cross-reactivity in which the body's infection-fighting cells misidentify the tissues of their own body with parts of the invading bacterium, and then, in a thoroughly inappropriate and devastating fashion, attack the heart, brain, skin, joints, and other major organs. Acute rheumatic fever most commonly presents itself in children between the ages of five and fifteen, yet it can and does occur occasionally in adults. As if its initial episode were not bad enough, subsequent infections with the streptococcal bacterium are usually far worse, reactivating these already damaged tissues and causing further inflammatory complications.[37] One speculation is that Chopin suffered from a damaging sequela of this disease that caused the permanent and progressive damage to one or more of his heart valves, eventually leading to his death from congestive heart failure. This possibility will be reviewed in greater detail in a subsequent chapter. Whether his correct diagnosis or not, rheumatic fever was common in those early times, with countless thousands suffering the consequences. Some thirty years earlier, Wolfgang Amadeus Mozart most likely had succumbed to kidney complications of rheumatic fever at the age of thirty-four. Illness spares no idols.

Others believe Chopin's infection was his first brush with tuberculosis, an event called *primary pulmonary tuberculosis*. This initial infection with the tubercle bacillus is customarily mild, often without any symptoms, yet it may start like a typical upper respiratory infection with sore throat, cervical lymph node swelling, fever, and cough. Recovery occurs spontaneously, and a protective immunity develops in most within a month or two. However, for a combination of reasons, some constitutional and others probably genetic, some individuals go on to develop a chronic form of the disease, termed *progressive tuberculosis*, an often torpid infection manifested by a constellation of vague symptoms of fever, loss of appetite, weight loss, and, of course, the cough. Could this have been the start of Chopin's lifelong illness?

Still others reject the foregoing hypotheses and postulate that Chopin's adolescent ailment was merely one of many rather ordinary respiratory infections the young composer would suffer over his lifetime. They argue that his symptoms were instead caused by the complications of cystic fibrosis, *bronchiectasis*, or other lung diseases. Regardless of just what his malady was, however, it took several months for the young man to recover, if indeed he really ever did manage to regain his full strength.

It appears likely, no matter which of the various hypotheses one favors, that Chopin's health took a significant blow during this episode. Following this illness, his concerned parents felt they needed to do something. As another of their children, Chopin's younger sister, Emilia, was also ill that year, they decided to send both away to the highly recommended health spa at Reinertz for a two-month stay. It would turn out to be a fortuitous decision for the young man. Chopin remained undaunted by the delicate state of his health and he pleasantly discovered that he possessed the remarkable ability to pen music of the utmost beauty and tranquility. Despite his isolation from his family and friends and his boredom with the spa's daily rituals, he managed to enjoy himself, taking leisurely hikes in the nearby scenic mountains, giving two very successful benefit concerts where he was delighted to perform his music, and generally was able to spend a relaxing summer. By that fall, he felt much improved.

Emilia Chopin (1812-1827).

Returning to Warsaw, Chopin needed to decide whether to proceed with a course of general education at the university, favored by his strait-laced father, or to pursue his own preference for more intensive musical study at the Warsaw Conservatory. Interestingly, after savoring the great success of his little concerts at Reinertz, he now seriously entertained a future in music. Quite typical of the ambiguity he felt at the time and of the pattern of uncertainty that would be repeated

throughout his life, and faced with his father's stringent recommenda-
tion, he decided to do both! By this time he had outdistanced any further efforts from the modest abilities of his first and forever-cherished
teacher, Żywny, and had linked up with a new musical instructor, Jósef
Elsner, the founder of the Warsaw Conservatory and the director of
opera at the National Theater. Like Żywny, Elsner was not a pianist,
and perceptively followed his predecessor's lead in similarly avoiding
any attempts at changing the young Chopin's unorthodox keyboard
style. Elsner, who would skillfully introduce the young prodigy to
music theory, studies on harmony, and counterpoint, quickly acknowledged his pupil to be a musical genius.[38]

Jóseph Elsner, Chopin's last music teacher.

Roughly two years after Chopin's summer stay at the Reinertz health spa, there were reports that another illness prompted his being rushed to a similar health spa at Sanniki, on the nearby estate of the Pruszak family.[39] Little is known about his brief stay there or the symptoms that prompted this treatment. In a letter written to Chopin's parents during their son's fairly brief stay at this spa, a mutual acquaintance by the name of Skrodzki reported that the young Chopin suffered from painful "dental cavities and gastric hyperacidity."[40] He also observed that Chopin's treatment regimen included generous allotments of ripe fruit and sweet wine, a pleasant and restorative remedy if there ever was one! Apparently nonplussed by his health difficulties, Chopin used this interlude to compose a charming trio for piano, violin, and cello. A Polish physician, Dr. Czeslaw Sielużycki, has suggested that this episode at Sanniki marked the ominous return of the young man's tubercular infection and the first sign of its inexorable advancement. This same physician claimed, without mentioning his sources, that the young Chopin also was "predisposed to rheumatic diseases, gastric troubles, severe headaches, and rotting teeth."[40] Some of these conclusions must be eyed cautiously.

Despite this brief setback, Chopin's Warsaw period was marked by his rapid ascent from his apprenticeship to the stardom of the concert stage, assisted, no doubt, by his composition of large bravura pieces for piano and orchestra. These works, among them the *Là ci darem Variations*, the *Fantasy on Polish Airs*, and his *Rondo à la Krokowiak*, became instant favorites with his audiences and served to expand exponentially his reputation as the musical darling of Poland. In short, he was becoming a big fish in a small pond. Already the pressure was increasing for him to move on to even greater challenges, but where? His two piano concertos, written during his final year at the Conservatory, were masterpieces by any standard, especially for having been written by a youth of nineteen. In their style and substance they were a quantum leap beyond his earlier orchestral works and would later serve to catapult the young man's reputation to international attention.

Fortunately, during this busy interval in Chopin's life in Warsaw there is no further record of any more health problems. He was able to pursue his ambitions without regard to his health. In a rather ebullient and boastful letter to his parents written during his brief 1829 stay in Vienna, he assured them, "...I am healthy and happy; eat and drink well."[41] Had he been significantly ill during this transitional phase of his life, his future most likely would have been profoundly different. He needed all the strength he could muster to weather the emotional storms of the tumultuous period he would spend between the time he left Warsaw and the time he finally arrived in Paris in 1831. Even with his apparent good health, Chopin lacked the temperament to decide his life's course at the close of his Warsaw studies, and remained susceptible to his often directionless and nebulous notions of a career, vacillating between the vocations of being either a professional pianist or full-time composer.

Through these years is the story of Chopin's circuitous journey from adolescent uncertainties to the self-confident independence of adulthood. He already had achieved a significant degree of stylistic individuality. He had achieved local recognition and fame in his hometown. Yet when he departed Warsaw for Vienna, he left his substantial support system behind. Once he found himself alone in this famed city of Mozart and Beethoven, a place preoccupied with its glorious past and rather indifferent to this unknown young man's emerging skills, he slipped into a period of loneliness and depression. His time there was marked by indecision and despair. In a letter to his good friend Jan Matuszyński in Warsaw, he wrote, "My parents tell me to please myself, and I don't want to go. To Paris? Here they advise me to wait. Return home? Stay here? — Kill myself? — Not write to you? Give me some advice, what to do. Ask the persons who dominate me, and write me their opinion, and so it shall be."[42] These are hardly the words of a confident man.

He had sought and, indeed, rather desperately needed recognition and reinforcement in Vienna, yet largely failed to achieve either due to his troubling self-doubt and inherent hesitancy to promote himself. He was genuinely rather shy and modest, not always the best attributes for one seeking his fame in the unsheltered public arena of the concert pianist. Although his performances in Vienna received generally favorable reviews, there would always be those critics who would complain that his tone was "too light," that his playing was embarrassingly inaudible for much of the audience. To the sensitive young composer, this discouraging criticism, however accurate, would greatly contribute to his indecision about a piano career and only add to his increasing dread of performing in public. This fear would only worsen. As Chopin once confided to Liszt, "I am not suited to public performances—the auditorium saps my courage, I suffocate in the exhalation of the crowd,

I am paralyzed by curious glances, and the sight of strange faces compels me to silence; but you, you were born to it." The swiftly maturing Chopin eventually left Vienna, inadvertently avoiding the advancing cholera epidemic and incrementally moving ever closer to his long-sought destination of Paris. Being in no particular rush to get there, he stopped in Stuttgart.

The unstable military and political situation in Poland at that moment only accentuated Chopin's sense of loss and isolation. The Warsaw forces, hopelessly outgunned and outnumbered, had been engaged in a protracted and bitter battle of resistance with the massive Russian occupation for some nine months. The Russians, led by the barbarous despot General Pashkievitch, ultimately prevailed, and Warsaw suddenly fell amid an intense and relentless fusillade of canon fire. Upon his hearing this terrible news after arriving in Stuttgart, Chopin essentially cracked, reacting hysterically and imagining the worst for his family and friends. The volcanic outburst he hastily scratched into his notebook after September 8, 1831, pages full of hallucinatory visions and visceral angst, was a raw testament to his soul's profound love for his Polish homeland.[43] This love for Poland was to become an overriding part of his persona, forever galvanized onto his psyche and indelibly translated into his music. After reading these written ravings, some have likened his mental state to schizophrenia, others to a manic-depressive state. I cannot agree. Given his proclivity to internal dramatic overreaction, his emotional instability of the preceding months, all compounded by his tremendous sense of isolation and no doubt aggravated by an excess of wine, his reaction was in character for the man. One need only listen to his music to savor the clues to his hair-trigger reactivity and understand this unusual man's capacity for emotional hyperbole.

Chopin's hesitancy to leave for Paris was most likely a psychological defense mechanism put into full play during this transitional time of his emotional upheaval. Admirably and rather inexplicably, he quickly collected himself, turned a blind eye to his ongoing indecisiveness, and determined on his own that his future success as a composer and a pianist lay in the City of Light. He left his homeland far behind, never to return, yet Poland's tragic plight would remain ever close to his heart.

In Paris and In Love

"Have a strong mind and a soft heart."
Anthony J. D'Angelo

Chopin's arrival in Paris in 1831 finally put an end to his protracted pilgrimage and his distressing battles with indecision. Armed with letters of introduction from influential people as well as a bolstered self-confidence, he quickly plunged into Parisian society and lost little time in the pursuit of his dream. The Paris he entered was then the cultural Mecca of the world, attracting the brilliant, the odd, and the simply daring, a world of stark contrasts and seemingly limitless possibilities. Chopin seemed dazed by the city's colorful array of unaccustomed sights: "There is the utmost luxury, the utmost swinishness, the utmost virtue, the utmost ostentation." His passably aristocratic bearing, his knowledge of the French language, and his reserved manner immediately facilitated his encounters with the members of the highest social circles. Also assisting with his acclimatization into French society were the members of the burgeoning Polish community in Paris, prominent among them the Czartoryskis, the Radziwiłłs, the beautiful singer and countess, Delfina Potocka, and the famous exiled Polish poet, Adam Mickiewicz. Through them Chopin would meet the renowned Baron de Rothchild, who would make the young man his favorite, assured of all the attendant privileges.[44] These and many more notables would become his true friends and loyal supporters. The November Uprising of 1830-1831 and the subsequent oppressive Russian occupation had led to a steady stream of Polish exiles heading to France, so that by the mid-1830s Paris would become a safe haven to a large cross-section of Polish society. Many of them would become deeply enamored with Chopin's often fervently revolutionary music, finding in it a common identity with their Polish patriotism and an incontestable boon to their cohesiveness as cultural exiles.

After being postponed four times, Chopin's first concert in Paris was held at the original Salle Pleyel on February 26, 1832. This beautiful hall, sumptuously decorated in the style of Louis XV, had been established by Camille Pleyel, then the leading piano manufacturer in France. Chopin greatly preferred the delicate and highly resonant tonal characteristics of Pleyel's pianos and would come to enjoy a lasting friendship with this successful entrepreneur. It must be remembered that at this time the concept of a solo piano concert did not exist. This form of individual artistic presentation would not be established until Franz Liszt's stunningly successful performance tour of Europe in 1840, during which he single-handedly introduced the reference standard still used to the present day. Thus, in Chopin's first public exposure in Paris, the concert included several musicians and works by many other composers. However, once Chopin took to the stage of the Salle Pleyel with his *Là ci darem Variations*, it was obvious he and his music had eclipsed all others at the concert. The Polish violinist Antoni Orlowski, in a letter written to his family, wrote, "All Paris was stupefied! Our Fritz mopped the floor with every one of the pianists here."[45] Although the famous hall was far from full, every important pianist in Paris had attended, including Liszt and Felix Mendelssohn, who both were leading the wild enthusiasm and praise for the young Pole's amazing talent.

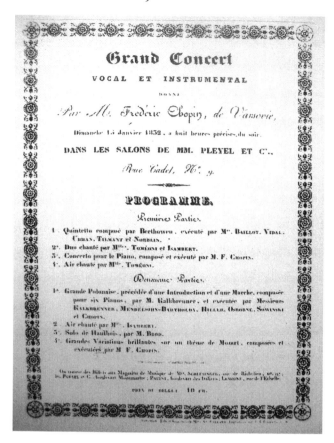

Flyer for Chopin's first concert in Paris.

With the intense spotlight of interest and curiosity shining on him, Chopin faultlessly made the most of it during his first years in Paris, clearly thriving with the adulation of his many admirers. His rapidly expanding repertoire of compositions now included polonaises, mazurkas, préludes, impromptus, études, waltzes, and ballades, all enthusiastically received and acclaimed. He was soon hailed as one of the best pianists if not *the* best in the world. His was a meteoric rise to stardom.

Without doubt, Chopin's études are the greatest instructional piano compositions yet penned. They address the most challenging technical difficulties through the use of masterful artistry of the highest order. In all, he wrote twenty-seven of them, the first set of *Op. 10* composed shortly after he reached Paris, with the rest published in 1833. Rather than regarding them as miniatures, they should be viewed as highly compressed forms capable of a virtual kaleidoscope of emotions.

Although they deal with the mundane mechanical problems encountered by all pianists, they are specifically designed for the virtuoso, and it certainly takes one to pull them off! They have managed to intimidate the very best, with Arthur Rubenstein recording nearly all of Chopin's works *except* them, and even the great Vladimir Horowitz shying away from a couple he claimed hurt his hands. These studies range in length from about a minute to over six and so are often performed as a set, much to the delight of discriminative audiences.

These first few years in Paris were to be some of the happiest times in the young Chopin's life. He had finally achieved what he had long sought—the recognition of his musical genius, reasonable financial independence, and the respect and admiration of many. This high regard brought with it not only fame but, perhaps even more importantly, new pupils, whose rather exorbitant lesson fees were to pay for Chopin's increasingly lavish tastes in clothing and socializing. However, this veneration would someday also bring to him the attention of another, one of the most controversial and prolific novelists of the nineteenth century, the intriguing George Sand. Chopin's fateful meeting with the clever French novelist, however, would not take place until 1836.

Meanwhile, he experienced a joyful reunion with his parents and the subsequent inception of an intensely romantic relationship with an old childhood friend. Chopin and his parents met at Carlsbad, Germany, during the summer of 1835, their first reunion since his departure from Warsaw, for a month of undiminished happiness. "Our joy," wrote Chopin, "is indescribable."[46] As they parted, not knowing this would be their last time together, Chopin penned what would become his favorite waltz, the entrancing *A flat Waltz, Op. 34, no. 1*, a piece full of warmth and elegance, yet coupled with elements of the nostalgia and melancholy so characteristic of many of his works. On his return to Paris, he passed through Dresden, where he unexpectedly ran into the Wodzińskis, a Polish family well known to him from his childhood, who were there visiting their relatives in Germany. His subsequent meeting with their sixteen-year-old daughter, Maria, took him entirely by surprise, as the last time he had seen her she was a mere toddler and he a teenager. In the meantime, Maria had grown to be an enticingly attractive and accomplished young lady and, to Chopin's further amazement, a highly proficient pianist. It really was love at first sight for both, and soon their mutual attraction would lure them into an even deeper relationship. Before his requisite departure to Paris, Chopin would write a lovely musical memento dedicated to her (*Waltz in A flat, Op. 69, no. 1*).

Maria Wodzińska.

The issue of Chopin's health became a major dilemma during his relationship with Maria. The Wodzińskis, very much aware of their only daughter's sudden infatuation, now cast a far more critical eye at her young Polish suitor, and what they saw must have been disconcerting. First, Chopin's heritage was common. He was not a member of the nobility they so proudly and ostentatiously represented. Second, he was a musician, a trade widely considered at the time to be of secondary consequence and having only limited socioeconomic potential. And lastly, and this may have been the deciding factor for them, was the uncertain state of Chopin's health. Although the specifics of his health are not recorded in the surviving correspondence of the time, reading between the lines and ascertaining the great caution expressed by the Wodzińskis over their daughter's possible future with Chopin gives the distinct impression that he must have appeared frail, if not already chronically ill.

Although Chopin's pleasant sojourn at the Wodzińkis' comfortable home was relatively brief, there still was sufficient time for Maria herself to observe the telltale signs of precarious health in her cherished beau. She would write to him to remind him not to forget to use his specially prepared cough remedies every night, while at the same time she would write privately to others of her incessant worries that beneath Chopin's throat and coughing problems there lurked a more serious and generalized disorder.[47] The Wodzińskis all probably had been aware of his reputation as a somewhat sickly person from their numerous contacts in Poland. Now, they would base their judgment also on what they themselves had observed that summer. They were increasingly concerned. As it would turn out, their fears were not unfounded.

Watercolor of Chopin by Maria Wodzińska.

A month later, back in Paris, Chopin became seriously ill, this time with bronchitis. The course of his illness was once again prolonged, and he experienced a further setback in November, coughing blood and suffering febrile hallucinations. His prolonged and very private recovery kept him so sequestered from his friends and family, it was widely rumored that he had died. To quell the rising flood of concern, the *Warsaw Courier* felt obligated to publish an announcement that following January, a correction to its previous printing of the rumors of the composer's death: "We wish to inform the many friends and admirers of the eminent talent of the virtuoso Frédéric Chopin, that the reports of his death which are circulating are without foundation."[48] Chopin was so frightened by this close scrape with death that he composed his will. Quite significantly, and perhaps for the first time in his life, his illness succeeded in reducing his prodigious musical output to a trickle.

Bronchitis is a common ailment. In fact, acute bronchitis is often an annoying yet unproblematic accompaniment to the common cold. Bronchitis lasting weeks or months, associated with high fever, hallucinations, and bleeding, the latter medically known as *hemoptysis,* is far more unusual, and in Chopin's case likely represented much more serious pathology. Again, tuberculosis is a leading possibility, if in fact he had been previously infected. However, his illness could have been a complication of cystic fibrosis, an inherited condition manifested by repeated and progressive respiratory infections. It might also have been simply his first experience with *bronchiectasis*, an abnormal widening and thickening of the bronchial tubes caused by the damage from multiple past infectious insults. By this time, it had become readily apparent to him, his family, and his friends that he was unduly vulnerable to respiratory infection and its complications. Whatever its cause, it was serious, and it initiated the frequent cycles of vigilant observation of his health status by an ever-widening circle of worried friends. What would begin as their mere concern would later progress to become their morbid curiosity as his health steadily deteriorated. Over time, most of his friends would become inured to his frailty and increasingly frequent episodes of incapacity.

Chopin's next visit with Maria, in the fall of 1836, proceeded so well that it led to his formal engagement to the charming young girl. Nearly simultaneously, it prompted her alarmed parents to impose a sort of probation on the couple's romantic plans. The Wodzińskis were determined to protect what matters they envisioned to be in their daughter's best interests, regardless of her rhapsodical infatuation with the young musician.

Frédéric and Maria were on another page. Rather unrealistically, Chopin entertained the comforting prospect of a return to his beloved Poland to assume the roles of both husband and piano teacher. He cherished the image of living a pastoral existence back in his homeland, a simpler life that would allow him the unlimited freedom to compose. Maria's mother, siding with the lovebirds as much as she dared, wrote to the young composer, "Rest assured that I am on your side, but we must take precautions if my wishes for you are to be fulfilled...Take care of your health, if all is to be well."[49] What then followed was her long laundry list of do's and don'ts containing detailed exhortations such as "wearing woolen stockings with your slippers," and inappropriately restrictive bedtime recommendations. Never one to follow such arbitrary constraints, Chopin, then *the* social butterfly of Paris, blissfully ignored that advice and continued with his deeply ingrained habit of late-night socializing and music-making, much to the mounting chagrin and resentment of Maria's worried parents.

That winter, Chopin succumbed once more to a series of similar respiratory infections, a seasonal pattern that would follow him for the rest of his life. It soon became clear from the surviving correspondence between Chopin and the Wodzińskis that his chances to wed the beautiful Maria would be forever thwarted by Maria's parents' rapidly growing misgivings about the stability of his health. Their final decision ended the young couple's relationship quickly and quietly. Chopin, predictably devastated and despondent, bundled up his many love letters from Maria, tying them with a ribbon, and labeled them, "Moja bieda" ("My trouble"). It's doubtful he ever read them again.

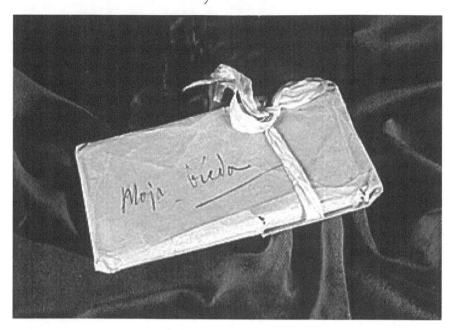

Chopin's letters from Maria, "Moja bieda," ("My trouble").

Despite being befriended by many of the aristocratic elite, Chopin had suffered the humiliation of being rejected by a respected count's daughter and from then on was destined never to become an esteemed landowner or one of their number. Although by then he had reached the pinnacle of artistic accomplishment, he never would achieve the impressive financial success of famous opera composers or of virtuoso pianists performing for huge crowds in the great concert halls. His pride profoundly wounded and his feelings deeply hurt, Chopin would carefully preserve these letters to the end of his life. The lovely Maria, the one true love of his life, was now gone, forever lost, along with his one opportunity to acquire the longed-for stability of an aristocratic status. This painful episode would be just another example of how his disease would so seriously alter his existence.

Simultaneous with this loss came the unexpected and pivotal meeting in Paris with George Sand. Psychologists might endlessly debate the details, yet it was obvious that the first encounter between Chopin and Sand came directly on the heels of his rebound from his recent relationship with Maria. Sand was well aware of this painful breakup and lengthily debated whether to pursue her attraction to the young composer, sharing intimate details and expounding her choices in her exuberantly verbose style in letters to both her friends as well as his. However, within a month, Chopin was confiding in his journal, "She understood me...she loves me." He was smitten once again.

Sand's sudden entry into Chopin's life coincided exactly with the deterioration of his hopes for marriage to Maria and his recovery from another lengthy episode of a serious illness. It marked the origin of a fateful relationship that sprang up with remarkable swiftness during one of the most vulnerable moments in the young composer's existence. His reaction to the abrupt shock over the loss of Maria and his subsequent emotional fragility must have contributed to his rather self-delusional response in overcoming his mixed initial reactions to the mysteries of the androgynous yet beguiling novelist. How his life would proceed from this point on was anyone's guess.

Chopin's Years with Sand

"When love is not madness, it is not love."
Pedro Calderon de la Barca

George Sand, the name Aurore Dupin Dudevant had crafted as her authorial pseudonym for her voluminous body of writing, was a truly remarkable woman. Well born, well educated, and a prolific author of novels and political tracts, she had achieved a reputation ranking her among the great writers of her day. Indeed, she was the most famous woman in France at the time she and Chopin first met in October 1836. Sand would remain well known until her death but, unlike Chopin's fame that would only continue to increase with time, hers would peak during her lifetime and then begin a long slide into relative obscurity. Marcel Proust, Dostoevsky, and many others highly admired her works, yet some, such as the great yet troubled French poet Charles Baudelaire, were much less kind: "She is stupid, she is ponderous, and she is long-winded."[50] Remarking on Sand's penchant for dressing in male attire, smoking cigars, and her habitual swearing in public, the American novelist, Henry James, once said, "She may be a man, but she's no gentleman."[51]

George Sand, dressed in her male attire.

Sand's influence on Chopin is still debated to this day, with opinions divided as to whether she aided or aggrieved him. More than likely, she accomplished both. By the time she met Chopin, some six years her junior, she had been romantically involved with a long list of men, and with all of them she acted in a primarily predatory and exploitative way. Sand and Chopin were nearly polar opposites in countless ways. She was descended from nobility, yet took the side of the common man; he arose from far more humble origins, yet his friends were of the aristocracy. He was fastidious; she was messy. He was nearly asexual; she was profligate with her sexual favors. While he was a musician of the highest order, she much preferred the written word to the musical score. And while Chopin's childhood had been a most pleasant, nearly carefree, and happy time, Sand's was marred by terrible loneliness and overwhelming despair. The thirty-four-year-old Sand and the twenty-eight-year-old Chopin became lovers in the spring of 1838. He never proposed to her and she never protested. Separately, they were each fascinating individuals with uniquely individual skills. Together, they were a study of enormous contrasts. Nearly inexplicably, they were to be paired for the next nine years.

What became pleasantly obvious was that Sand's presence in Chopin's life in no way interfered with his ability to compose. Fortunately, he possessed an amazing attention span with vigorous powers of concentration, allowing him to fathom his inner resources and continue with his work, regardless of her attendance or other external stimuli, and whether experiencing good health or bad. Their social calendar became a busy one and often included the who's who of Paris at the time. Under Sand's influence, the intimate circle of Chopin's friends that included the painter Eugène Delacroix, the cellist Auguste Franchomme, and musicians Liszt and Hector Berlioz, widened to embrace the poets Heinrich Heine and Adam Mickiewicz, the writer Honoré de Balzac, and a long list of other influential personalities.

An early photograph of George Sand.

Despite the oppressive heat, they spent their first summer together living in Paris, not going to Sand's comfortable ancestral home in Nohant, as would become their custom in future years. By that fall, Sand was determined to take her two young children somewhere to the south, especially considering that her young son, Maurice, supposedly suffered from some sort of painful arthritic disorder and an enlargement of his heart. Convinced by the prospects for an ideal climate and an affordable stay, she eventually settled on finding a place on the island of Majorca, just off Spain's east coast in the Mediterranean, and then spent countless weeks trying to persuade the reluctant Chopin to accompany her and her children. Although initially hesitant, his recurrent coughing had again become so serious in the damp cold of Paris that he and his friends soon became convinced it was imperative he join his new family. Liszt was greatly alarmed at the deteriorating state of his friend's health and strongly urged him to leave the city for a warmer and possibly healthier climate. Acting discreetly in order to avoid any extra gossip over his rather unaccountable and curiously clandestine relationship with Sand, Chopin quietly departed for Majorca. He could not have predicted his journey's frightening consequences.

The three months Chopin and Sand spent in Majorca were to become a difficult and disheartening chapter in the engaging story of their lives. Not only was Chopin forced to assume the awkward position of father and husband to those he really didn't know very well, he had to contend with a dramatic worsening of his physical condition. To his eternal credit, despite all his turmoil and suffering, he rather miraculously managed to continue composing, completing two nocturnes, writing the *Ballade in F major, Op. 38*, the *Scherzo in C-sharp minor, no. 3, Op. 39*, and finishing his astonishingly beautiful *Twenty-four Préludes, Op. 28*.

Stylized painting of George Sand.

It is claimed by some musicologists that there are few examples of Chopin's works that can be accurately linked to any particular event in his life. I strongly disagree. One of the obvious examples of just how significantly the character of his work was influenced by external events can be heard in the *Prélude in D minor*, the fourth of the *Op. 28* set. Written during his disastrous visit to Majorca, it opens with a morbidly melancholic tone and then quickly goes downhill from there. Chopin apparently often performed it himself, and it was played again at his funeral. If ever despair was printed in notes, this was it.

The newly formed family eventually found lodging, some twenty miles north of the town of Palma at the abandoned and partially ruined Carthusian monastery at Valldemossa, a medieval stone structure remotely located up in the rugged hills overlooking the sea, but not without first experiencing some frustrating difficulties. Sand had initially tried to obtain rooms for them in Palma but had no success. As she wrote later, "It was impossible to find in the entire town even one habitable apartment. An apartment in Palma is composed of four absolutely naked walls, without windows or doors. In most bourgeois homes, glass windows are not used and when one wishes to secure such a delicacy, it has to be constructed...His successor is forced to start by replacing them, unless he enjoys living in the wind, which is a taste greatly accepted by Palma."[52] Chopin also found himself without a piano, as the one he had ordered from Paris had not arrived and, as his custom was to compose only with the instrument, he was exceedingly frustrated. As he wrote to his Paris friend and piano manufacturer, Camille Pleyel, "I dream of music, but I do not play..."

The trip had been difficult enough thus far, but then the rains came, and things got even worse. Not only was it a deluge, it was also cold. Chopin's coughing steadily worsened and eventually led to the consultation from the island's practitioners previously described. Their combined opinion, however poor their skills and rudimentary their medical knowledge, was that Chopin was consumptive and seriously ill. Soon thereafter, word quickly spread that there was a foreigner seriously infected with tuberculosis living in the community, effectively closing all of the local stores to the family's basic needs and prompting their panic-stricken landlord to send a letter of eviction to the struggling party. In it, he demanded immediate payment to cover the disinfection of the entire villa, the burning of Chopin's bed and bedclothes together with his treasured little Pleyel piano, and the repainting and refurbishment of the entire apartment. Besieged not only by his deepening cough and his increasingly apprehensive neighbors, Chopin also had to contend with intestinal distress. In a letter to his longstanding friend and Polish compatriot, Wojciech Grzymała, he wrote, "I feel weak, my friend. I have a sort of diarrhea."[53] Although some medical researchers have attempted to link this episode of gastrointestinal distress to the malabsorption syndrome accompanying cystic fibrosis or the intestinal pathology of tuberculosis, others simply attribute Chopin's problem to his intolerance of the high fat content and garlic in the typical Majorcan cuisine. It may have been a food-borne gastroenteritis. Any firm conclusion is impossible. Whatever its cause, Chopin's condition was suddenly becoming critical.

What had begun as a poetically lovely holiday repose under the sunny skies of paradise, holding the potential for being a necessary healing and bonding interlude for Chopin, Sand, and her children, had turned into a living nightmare. Now, they were forced to leave. Summing up their experience at Majorca, Sand penned, "Our stay at the Valldemossa monastery was therefore a punishment for him and a torment for me."[54]

Their misery didn't end as they left the island. Rushed to take the first boat leaving Majorca, they were aghast to discover that the ship was already loaded with a large herd of pigs. Sensing his feeble passenger's potential for contagion, the frightened captain pitilessly restricted Chopin to a small squalid room below deck, steaming hot and filled with the stench of the surrounding noisy animals. Apparently, it was then the queer custom for the mariners to whip the pigs during the sea crossing in an attempt to keep them from getting seasick, so the frightened animals were constantly squealing. Chopin was soon coughing and spitting basins of blood.

Arriving in Barcelona the next day, he was attended by a sympathetic doctor from a French warship and a friend of Sand's, a Jacques Coste, who somehow helped stop the composer's bronchial hemorrhaging. As there were no direct means of doing that at the time, I suspect the good doctor turned to the time-trusted remedy of administering opium to subdue Chopin's cough reflex. Resting a week in Barcelona, the four eventually sailed to Marseilles where the esteemed physician Dr. Cauvières gave the composer hope that there were no tubercular foci in his lungs. Chopin finished his *F major Ballade,* composed the *B flat minor Sonata* with its "funeral march," and also hurriedly penned a few mazurkas. Slowly heading north through Arles, the now-rested family eventually found its way back to Nohant, where Chopin improved steadily.

While the events of his island stay were dramatic and frightening, none of Chopin's symptoms at Majorca are specific enough for any particular diagnosis. There may be a few helpful clues, however. His coughing combined with the bleeding (hemoptysis) can be compatible with several conditions aside from tuberculosis, although the large amount of bleeding may be unusual for those with cystic fibrosis or other conditions such as alpha 1-antitrypsin deficiency (there will be more discussion about these illnesses later). His high fevers that were at times combined with hallucinatory behavior point toward an infectious cause to his illness, although that cannot be considered in any way diagnostic. However, the hypothesis that Chopin may have suffered from valvular heart disease as a consequence of his possible adolescent bout with rheumatic fever appears much less likely with this episode, as it would not have been expected for the hemoptysis or hemorrhagic coughing to occur with such severity so early in the course of his illness. Furthermore, the pulmonary hypertension resultant from some types of valvular heart disease is usually a late finding in the course of these problems and would not be seen in a person who would continue to live for another decade.[55]

No matter if the events at Majorca do little to change our analysis of Chopin's disease, they rather suddenly did change the dynamics of the already tempestuous relationship between Chopin and Sand. What had begun only a year earlier as the passionate yet odd attraction between two famous personalities quickly metamorphosed into something quite radically different. Sand would from then on assume a strongly maternal bearing, an accustomed role she would continue to play for the remaining years of their friendship. She would henceforth view Chopin as an invalid, nearly another of her children, her most common name for him being "my little one." Whatever sexual attraction may have existed in those initial ethereal weeks of their courtship quickly evaporated into the cosmos, forever lost.

Once back in Paris, Chopin's condition gradually improved. Once again, his physicians wanted to bleed him, but as he mentions in a letter to his good friend and helper, Julian Fontana, "I did not let them, or rather that they were not permitted, to bleed me; that I wear vessicants (sic) [agents inducing blisters], that I am coughing very little in the morning, and that I am not yet looked upon as a consumptive person. I drink neither coffee nor wine, but milk. Lastly, I keep myself warm, and look like an old woman."[56]

He continued composing, putting the finishing touches on his *Ballade in F, Op. 38*, several mazurkas, and his *Scherzo in C-sharp minor, Op. 39*. This latter work may be yet another of Chopin's works that mirrored his personal situation. It's a stunning feat of composition. Composed of two highly contrasting musical ideas that never are allowed to intersect or combine, I believe it represents the pattern of the discordant relationship he was then experiencing with Sand. That following summer, he and Sand were back at Nohant, where he never before as an adult had experienced such comfort. Sand's family estate, while not exactly a castle, is a large, spacious, and comfortable home, surrounded by beautiful park-like gardens and innumerable large trees.

It proved to be a perfect place for him to escape the bustle and pollution of the big city and find the time for composing. Many of Chopin's biographers attribute his continued success at composition, despite his chronic health problems, to his spending several idyllic summers at Nohant. They also credit Sand for her constant loving care and attendance to his many needs. For all her efforts, Sand's only insistence was that he show up at mealtimes and enjoy the company of her children. Chopin readily complied and came to know her two children well, especially the coquettish adolescent, Solange. Sadly, there would be importunate consequences to their rather ambiguous connection. His complicated friendship and possible intimacy with this beautiful yet manipulative young girl would, in a series of complicated incidents, eventually lead to the denouement in his relationship with Sand.

After the tranquil and at times monotonous summer months at Nohant, Chopin longed to return to the excitement and stimulation of Paris. He thoroughly enjoyed attending the opera, the theater, and being back in his apartment instructing his many pupils. He desperately needed the income he derived from teaching. Throughout the first months of 1840, Chopin would teach for long hours in a sustained effort to improve his financial position after suffering the disastrous expenses of Majorca. Perhaps due to his active tutorage, there appears to be another lull in his musical composition. Despite the sad fact that none of his nearly 150 students ever achieved fame, by all accounts he was an excellent instructor.

While reasonably profitable, his hectic teaching schedule kept him sufficiently occupied and, combined with his typical predilection for cold-weather illness, it eventually became impossible for him to compose during the winter months. His energies then were largely directed toward his students. Most of his pupils were talented amateurs; few were children, with two remarkable exceptions. One was Karl Filtch, a highly skilled German-Hungarian boy of eleven, and the other was Adolf Gutmann, a German lad of fifteen who was to become Chopin's favorite. It was claimed that both of these students were excellent pianists. Although Karl had been Chopin's pupil for less than two years, he learned quickly and so well that his proud teacher boasted he would give up performing once his young prodigy began his concertizing career. Tragically, Filtch would never live to achieve that illusory goal, dying of tuberculosis at the age of fifteen. Gutmann's career never launched either, yet he would become a trusted friend and would later be present to cradle Chopin's head in his hands as the composer drew his last breath.

Karl Filtch, Chopin's "best" pupil.

While in Paris, Chopin and Sand managed their quite different lifestyles by living apart in separate yet conveniently nearby apartments, except for those times he was ill, when he would then retreat to her restful home for her comforting ministrations. It was obvious to all that the couple's relationship had changed drastically. Always civil to one another, their times together more and more resembled the relationship of a mother and son, nurse and patient. By the time he was thirty in 1840, Chopin's health was already in steady decline. He coughed nearly continually: "I cough and do nothing." He suffered frequent fevers and appeared weakened. His spirits, rather surprisingly, appeared generally bright despite his infirmity. Nevertheless, his closest friends knew he was merely concealing his melancholy behind a guise of gaiety. And, of course, he continued composing.

For such a highly regarded and celebrated pianist, Chopin gave very few public concerts. In all, there were only about thirty of them.[57] Where he did perform and where his reputation largely originated and then continued, were in the private salons of Paris, intimate settings for the adoring few. He would consent to his rare public concert appearances only after extended pleas from his closest friends. Increasingly hesitant to expose himself to any possible criticism, and cognizant of his physical frailty that compromised his already muted playing, he desperately wished to stay out of the limelight. Finally acquiescing to these many entreaties, he reluctantly consented to perform his next concert in April of 1841.

In a letter to their close friend and famous Parisian singer, Pauline Viardot, Sand wrote of Chopin's pre-concert nervousness, "So many things frighten him that I proposed he play without candles and without the auditorium on a mute piano." Despite her playful teasing and his incessant fretting, the concert was held at the newly constructed Salle Pleyel, located only a few blocks away from the original hall where he had performed to such acclaim in 1832. In his flowery prose, Liszt wrote a lengthy account of the event, describing everything from the flowers draped over the stairs leading to the hall to what attire those who attended chose to wear before eventually proceeding to portray the main attraction of the evening. "He has seldom allowed himself to be heard in public; the eminently poetic nature of his talent is not suited to that. Similar to those flowers which open their fragrant calyces only in the evening, he requires an atmosphere of tranquility and composure in order to yield up the melodic treasures which repose within him…the muse of his homeland dictates his songs, and the anguished cries of Poland lend to his art a mysterious, indefinable poetry which, for all those who have truly experienced it, cannot be compared to anything else."[58] For the four hundred guests in attendance, it was a night to remember, a grand success. For his part, Chopin was relieved to have the ordeal over.

The following year, Chopin cautiously agreed to yet another concert, this one also to be held at the Pleyel hall. Again, he played magnificently, the event being an astounding success, artistically as well as financially. Yet with all his stress in preparing for the event and the concert itself, he afterwards claimed exhaustion and spent weeks recuperating in bed, additionally complaining of a sore throat and an aching mouth. At times it was difficult for Sand to remain sympathetic as she suspected some of his ills to be hypochondriacal. After all, his recent physicians in both Nohant and Paris had pronounced him free from consumption, so what was she to believe? More than likely, there was also an element of denial in both Sand and Chopin when it came to facing the inevitable prospect of a fatal illness. In the absence of any firm diagnosis, their acceptance of a nebulous psychophysiological disorder may have fit their need to explain away many of his symptoms. However, their psychological denial mechanisms were dealt a serious blow when they learned of the terminal condition of Jan Matuszyński, a close Polish friend, doctor, and former schoolmate of Chopin. Jan would die a painfully slow and agonizing death from tuberculosis, as had so many others of Chopin's friends. At that moment, the deadly reality of his disease probably hit home for the frail composer and most likely was an unforgettable emotional blow from which he never fully recovered.

Rather amazingly, Chopin's star status was still in the ascendancy. Despite his increasing physical debility, his fame only continued to grow and spread. Fatefully, for another few years, his musical capacities were also spared. In the early 1840s, his powers of melodic invention, harmonic complexity, and composition were at their peak. What followed were the masterpieces of his mature period, the magnum opus of the *B minor Sonata*, the powerful *Scherzo in E*, the lilting *Berceuse* and the *Barcarolle*, and the formidable *Ballade in F minor*. The popularity of this complex work has now surpassed that of the venerable *Op. 38*, the so-called *Third Ballade*. One of the most interesting works of Western music, it achieves a transcendent level of sophistication and artistry. I am convinced his last *Ballade,* a work employing all of his remarkable gifts for inventiveness and composition, expresses a sort of summation of his life and a resigned and fatalistic acceptance of his death. Together, these jewels of the piano literature would forever establish Chopin's legacy in the world of Western music, as they would continue to win well-deserved praise from amazed and delighted audiences to the present day.

Chopin at the piano.

In addition to these larger forms, he also continued to write the diminutive pieces that were his favorite. Never far from his heart were his mazurkas, probably the most personal and chromatically radical music he ever penned. He never tired of writing them and always obtained joy in performing them. Some of his greatest, three in each of his *Op. 50* and *Op. 56*, were to be written during the same few years. The inventive chromaticism and unusual rhythms of these works would have far-reaching consequences, as they influenced many of the works of the major composers of the nineteenth and twentieth centuries, including Wagner, Brahms, Scriabin, Debussy, and Ravel.

By the mid-1840s, Chopin's abilities, now mental as well as physical, were in decline, never to recover. He remained busy, yet struggled to compose. His output of the time included several waltzes, nocturnes, and mazurkas, and, perhaps most notably, his *Sonata in G minor* for cello and piano, a moving work, harboring, as with so many of his works, a distinctly autobiographical slant. Written during the years

1845-1846, its opening movement begins with chords taken directly from Franz Schubert's gloomy song-cycle, *Winterreise*, one of that composer's final works written just prior to his death from syphilis in 1828.[59] The story of how this work influenced the steadily weakening Chopin is interesting.

Schubert's song begins with the tale of a heartbroken young man, rejected by his true love and aimlessly wandering, lost in a bitterly cold winter wilderness. Chopin had composed his cello and piano sonata at a difficult time in his life, when his relationship with Sand was seriously strained. His physical incapacities had reduced his position in the Sand household to that of no more than a visiting sick relative. Increasingly, there were differences of opinion as to how to raise the children, who by this time had grown into rather willful souls frequently at odds with their mother. Sand struggled to tolerate her childrens' unruly antics and the composer's increasingly dependent physical needs. The somber character of Chopin's lovely sonata echoes the dissonance of his domestic problems as well as his reflections on his advancing disease, and mirrors the mood of Schubert's twenty-four song cycle about rejection and death.

Chopin's rejection by Sand might be demonstrated by his use of the opening chords of Schubert's *Winterreise* in his cello and piano sonata, a work he never brought himself to play in its entirety in public. At one of his last concerts, the memorable Paris concert of 1848, held the year after Chopin's and Sand's eventual break, he was scheduled to begin the second half of the program with this work, yet he suddenly collapsed just prior to his returning to the stage. Eventually, he roused himself and returned to perform but mysteriously omitted the first movement. Possibly, he was embarrassed that his musically sophisticated audience might recognize his musical quote from Schubert's piece and link its bleak story to the painful chapter of his recent brouhaha with Sand. This exceedingly sensitive composer, always attuned to the slightest innuendo or gossip, did not wish to make public that painful episode in his life.

The exact reasons for Chopin's final break with Sand remain elusive. The series of events leading to their separation became very complex, full of intrigue and personal folly. It's probably correct to assume that George Sand, never a sit-at-home type, had felt increasingly burdened by her maternal duties in caring for the infirm composer and resented her life being languished away in the sickroom of her one-time lover. Most likely, she felt it was time to move on and impatiently awaited the right moment. That turning point would come during a family dispute that provoked Sand's strong opposition to her daughter Solange's impending marriage to a rather wild opportunist, the second-rate sculptor, Auguste Clésinger. While Chopin never particularly cared for Clésinger (nor his sculptures), he was quite close to Solange and somewhat naively chose to support the young couple in their love, opposing Sand. Solange's sudden announcement of her pregnancy and her subsequent throwing of herself into an icy river in a vain attempt at an abortion, were still not sufficient to trump her mother's rejection of her impending marriage to the purportedly alcoholic Clésinger. Matters finally came to physical blows between the temperamental sculptor and the enraged novelist of Nohant, with the evicted and embarrassed young lovers hastily fleeing to Paris in Chopin's carriage.

At the time far removed in Paris and knowing none of these sordid details, Chopin quite innocently had previously lent the young couple that carriage. Sand was outraged. She considered his assistance to her now-estranged daughter to be an inappropriate interference into the personal affairs of *her* family, and she never would forgive him for it. Chopin had been the perplexed yet passive observer of this distant soap opera, only days later receiving word of Sand's splenetic rejection in a terse letter: "Farewell, my friend! May you be healed quickly of all your ailments, and I hope for it now (I have my reasons for that), and I shall thank God for this bizarre denouement of nine years of exclusive friendship. Give me your news occasionally. It is useless ever to return to the rest."[60] They never did. They were to have only one last brief and perfunctory encounter shortly following the birth of Solange's child.

At the start of their relationship, Chopin was an apparently healthy young man on his way up the ladder of success and fame. By the end of it, he had been reduced to the position of a semi-invalid, his art all but lost. Increasingly frustrated by his inability to compose, he would cry out, "Where has my Art gone?" He was now a depressed and broken man, rejected by yet another love in his life and facing a very uncertain future. Chronically ill, unable to teach or make a living, deprived of the comfort and support he had received for so long from Sand, he was now alone and nearly destitute. Fortuitously, help was soon to arrive.

Decline and Death

"Your vision will become clear only when you look into your heart. Who looks outside, dreams. Who looks inside, awakens."
Carl Jung

Chopin spent that winter anxiously waiting for news from Sand, still not giving up his hope for their reconciliation, an accord he would never live to see. What energy he possessed he conserved for teaching, and he enjoyed middling success in attracting a few new pupils. One of them, Jane Stirling, a single woman six years older than Chopin and only a fledgling pianist, began to occupy an increasingly prominent role in his life. The daughter of a wealthy Scottish shipping magnate, she had come to Paris in search of a singing career and, after a chance meeting with the composer, began to become increasingly enamored with both Chopin's artistic accomplishments and the man himself. She was especially impressed by his modesty, his stoical attitude in the face of his serious illness, and, of course, his playing. Stirling would come to play a critically important role in the months ahead.

It was the time of the 1848 French Revolution, a bold attempt by the liberal establishment and reform movement to change the course of the country. After witnessing a precipitous economic decline and enduring a subsequent severe depression, the French people were primed for a change in their government. The Revolution would bring an end to the reign of King Louis-Philippe and his fellow elites, and marked the creation of the French Second Republic.[61] Universal suffrage, restoration of the freedom of the press, and unemployment relief were the first things on the new regime's agenda and quickly gained widespread support. Disillusionment would come later, but at that moment the country was swept up in the enthusiasm for the impending radical change in the social order. Chopin, rather characteristically, was repelled by politics and paid scant attention to these affairs, aside from casually observing the barricades in the streets. Preoccupied with his world of music, he failed to comprehend the effect the Revolution would have on his adopted country and his pupils, most of whom were established members of the aristocratic elite.

Given only days before the Revolution, Chopin's concert of that February, his last in Paris, proved to be a dramatic success and garnered ecstatic reviews despite his sudden collapse minutes before the start of the second half of the program. However, he somehow rallied to perform the last three movements of his *Sonata in G minor*, several preludes, mazurkas, and a waltz before basking in the warmth of the thunderous applause. It is not possible to reconstruct the exact program of the 1848 concert with certainty, although many have made valiant attempts at it. Three hundred seats were available, but many of the hall's best had been specifically reserved for the royals. However, due to the extreme political instability of the time and their fear of appearing in public, they failed to attend, and so their empty seats probably left a gaping hole in the audience that night. Inadvertently, and further contributing to the concert's reduced attendance, Chopin had rather fastidiously seen to it there wouldn't be any complimentary tickets, posters, or other advertising. Among other details, we know the audience begged for a repeat performance of his *Waltz in D flat*, an early work, yet one filled with a wonderful interweaving of melodic dance themes.

Almost immediately, there were hurried plans for a second follow-up concert, yet these were quickly dashed by the onset of the Revolution that was already in full swing within days of the fading memories of the first performance. A week after Chopin's final concert, thousands protesting the monarchy raced through the streets of Paris, with many brutally killed in the conflict that followed. The following day, the king reluctantly abdicated and, later that same night, surreptitiously fled the city. Cleverly disguised as an old woman, he only narrowly escaped apprehension.

Jane Wilhelmina Stirling (1804-1859).

A strong supporter of Louis-Philippe and a proud member of the cultured elite of Paris, Jane Stirling felt compelled by the changing political climate to leave France and return to London, and she kindly invited Chopin to join her that spring. Ambivalent as always, Chopin took some time to decide. Lacking direction in Paris, he sought a more stable existence, and with it, some possible opportunity for financial success. Before making his decision, he sought the medical approval of his newest physician, Dr. Molin, a practitioner of the newly established science of homeopathy. Chopin had credited Dr. Molin with saving his life the preceding winter after he suffered his usual series of respiratory exacerbations. Having become dissatisfied with the care he had received from his traditional physicians, and after the repeated urgings of Stirling and also those of Liszt, he instead had sought medical attention from several homeopathic practitioners, including his favorite, Dr. Molin. It was to be a fortunate choice.

Founded in the 1830s by Samuel Hahnemann, a previously unsuccessful German physician and translator, homeopathy attempted to combat disease without further weakening the patient.[62] Compared to the terrible array of traditional treatments of the time, a frightening collection that included emetics, toxic chemicals, blistering agents, hot irons, leeches, and bleeding, homeopathic medicine appeared to be a genuine advance, a scientific breakthrough. It was founded on the principle of what Hahnemann called, "the law of similars," a concept that claimed a particular illness could be cured by the use of drugs that created symptoms similar to those of the disease. By administering infinitesimally small doses of these matched agents, Hahnemann boldly claimed improvement was certain for most and cure possible for many. Although these diluted placebos undoubtedly did little good, Chopin's dependence on them allowed him to avoid certain harm. There can be little doubt that by shunning the wholly inadequate and often detrimental treatments advocated by the typical allopathic physicians of his day and turning to homeopathy, Chopin managed to prolong his life.

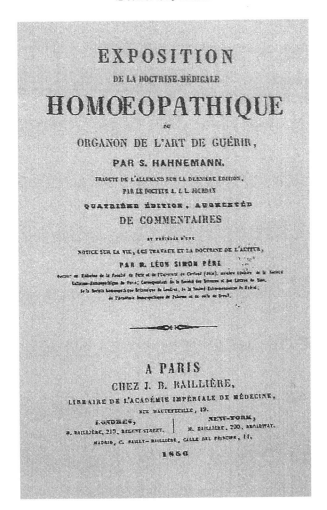

Daguerreotyoe of Samuel Hahnemann alongside the frontspiece of his treatise on homeopathy.

It would be erroneous to assume, however, that Dr. Hahnemann's homeopathic treatments consisted of only diluted placebos. Granted, the true homeopathic agents he administered were indeed without much actual effect, yet his medical arsenal also included agents of proven worth. These additional treatments he advocated provided therapeutic effectiveness as well as symptomatic relief. Quinine was used to reduce fever. Belladonna extract was used for its known ability to reduce copious chest secretions. Opium, that notable nostrum of old, when mixed into a flavored and sugary syrup, quickly became a godsend for the long-struggling composer. As Chopin once had written to Sand, "I believe the drug calms me very much…" In that same note, Chopin anxiously had reminded his wearying companion to obtain his homeopath's necessary authorization for yet another refill of this much-prized prescription. Over the next couple of years, he would have abundant justification to make good use of it.[63]

With none of his doctors opposed to his travel, Chopin set off for England in April of 1848. Jane Stirling's fastidious arrangements for her favored composer during his stay in London and his subsequent trip to Scotland were exceptionally complete, she and her accompanying sister paying close attention to his every need. Although he brought his favorite Pleyel piano with him, he was also provided with his choice of the best English pianos and, with them, managed to give several financially successful, if rather artistically compromised concerts.

While in the English capitol, Chopin found the time to consult with another homeopathic physician, a Dr. Lyszczynski, presumably because he needed a fresh source for a diminishing supply of his opium-laced cough cocktail.[64] Despite the sometimes overly attentive care he received, Chopin's feelings for the English were generally unfavorable, as he often felt they regarded his music as merely something to provide a decorous complement for their loud conversation, which at times was sufficiently noisy to drown out his vain attempts to be audible in the vast spaces of their concert halls. He went on to play public concerts in Manchester, Glasgow, Edinburgh, and at the stately homes of several wealthy friends of the Stirlings, and even another back in London for the queen, but he found himself increasingly miserable.

Chopin would begin to pen a flurry of increasingly frantic letters to his friends in Paris. To Camille Pleyel, he wrote, "I breathe with difficulty. I am entirely ready to kick the bucket."[65] In another, written to his favorite pupil, Adolf Gutmann, he complains, "Things are getting worse with me every day. I feel weaker; I cannot compose, not for want of inclination, but for physical reasons…I am all morning unable to do anything, and when I have dressed myself I feel again so fatigued that I must rest. After dinner, I must sit for two hours with the gentlemen, hear what they say in French, and then see how much they can drink. Meanwhile I feel bored to death…afterwards my good Daniel carries me upstairs to my bedroom, undresses me, puts me to bed, leaves the candle burning, and then I am again at liberty to sigh and dream until morning, to pass the day just like the preceding one."[66]

Despite Chopin's alarming frailty, the attentive Stirling, wishing to assume the role George Sand once played, chose to view Chopin as a potential mate, much to his shock and dismay. To his close Polish friend, Wojciech Grzymała, he confided, "I am closer to a coffin than a marriage bed."[67]

He returned to Paris in late November and made a determined if rather desperate effort to resume his teaching. As that task proved impossible, he instead set to work completing works he had previously left undone, including the *Mazurka in G minor,* the *Mazurka in F minor,* and his *Nocturne in E minor, Op. 72,* thought to be his last works. He occasionally attended the opera and once went for a lengthy carriage drive down the Champs-Elysées with his good friend, Delacroix, but after April 1849, when his health entered its crisis stage, his debility confined him to his apartment.

There was no end to the stream of well-wishers and friends who would drop by for a brief visit or to entertain him with their music-making. Lacking the ability to support himself financially and quickly running out of money, Chopin decided to leave his small yet expensive apartment at the square d'Orléans for cheaper lodgings and better air quality just outside the city on rue Chaillot. Although it was located at a distance far from many of his oldest friends, they still managed to visit him as frequently as ever. Hector Berlioz, the famous French composer and a good friend of Chopin's, often visited his colleague and, after one of visits, recalled, "…his weakness and sufferings had become so great that he could no longer either play the piano or compose; even the slightest conversation fatigued him in an alarming manner. He endeavored generally to make himself understood as far as possible by signs."[68] All could see how quickly he was failing. Alarmed by his faltering ability to speak, Chopin summoned for his older sister Ludwika, still in Warsaw, requesting her presence by his side as he now faced a certain death.

By that June, he was suffering more episodes of hemorrhagic coughing. Not improving, painfully aware that his trusted Dr. Molin had recently died, and bothered by recurrent diarrhea, he felt he needed to try a new approach, and so in July, after noting the onset of leg swelling, in rapid order he consulted four distinguished physicians despite their nearly unaffordable high fees. Several of them were noted specialists in tuberculosis, notably Dr. Jean-Gaston-Marie Blache, the president of the Academy of Medicine in Paris, and a Dr. Louis. Another was the highly renowned physician Dr. Jean Baptiste Cruveilhier, who had once served as physician to the French royal family, Talleyrand, and Francois-René de Chateaubriand, among other notable luminaries, and who, at the time, occupied the honored position of Chair of Pathologic Anatomy at the University of Paris. In fact, some considered him, "the best specialist in tuberculosis and pathology in Paris."[69] He had written several books on tuberculosis, pathology, and anatomy. His most famous publication was his *Anatomie Pathologique de Corps Humain*, a magnificent pathologic atlas still greatly revered to this day. Although a far stronger anatomist than a seasoned medical clinician, Cruveilhier became Chopin's most trusted physician during his last months, being with him all the way to the end. After Chopin's death, it would be Cruveilhier's responsibility to sign the death certificate and perform a limited postmortem examination while removing the composer's heart.

All of Chopin's recently chosen practitioners had become familiar with the stethoscope, the newly introduced and eventually important mainstay of medicine invented in 1816 by René-Théophile-Hyacinthe Laennec,[70] a physician at the Necker-Enfants Malade Hospital in Paris. The instrument's general acceptance by the medical establishment, however, did not materialize until the early 1840s. At that point in time, the stethoscope was a mere wooden tube, lacking the critically important amplification chamber and trumpet-like earpiece that would be introduced and refined only a few years later.[71] Nevertheless, its use proved to be a boon to physicians, improving the limited accuracy of their often vain efforts to understand the internal workings of the human body. The stethoscope was to become an especially important device in helping physicians detect disease in the lungs, yet at that time its contribution was debatable. In Chopin's case, the stethoscope's benefit was probably minimal, despite the acknowledged skills of its operators. Unfortunately, their findings often did more to confuse them than to offer helpful answers. The proper use of this soon-to-be-indispensable medical tool, currently so tied to the understanding of the mechanics of the heart and airflow through the lungs, would have to wait.

***Portrait of René-Théophile-Hyacinthe Laennec,
the inventor of the stethoscope.***

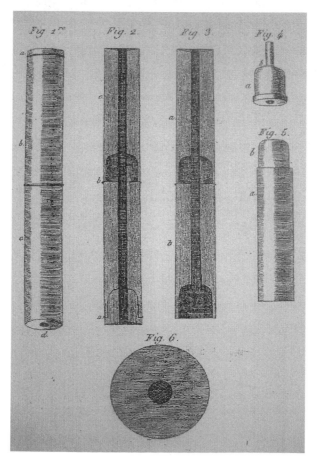

Early stethoscopes. Illustration of the primitive instrument.

However, the fact that these trained practitioners did not hear a murmur over his heart may indeed be important in our analysis of his disease. The physicians treating Honoré de Balzac (1799-1850), the famous French author who lived in Paris and who was Chopin's contemporary and acquaintance, through their use of the newly introduced stethoscope were able to detect the telltale sounds of an incompetent heart valve in their illustrious patient and then correctly ascribe his breathlessness and leg swelling to the valvular heart disease that later took his life. Balzac was in florid heart failure during the late 1840s, and his murmur provided an excellent clue as to its cardiac cause. This is strong testimony to the medical abilities of the time. Chopin's physicians, however, did not record their ever hearing such similar sounds during his many exams. To the contrary, their difficulties in hearing any abnormal sounds in their examinations of the composer's lungs led them to doubt the diagnosis of tuberculosis.

Honoré de Balzac, the famous French author.

Another auscultatory finding capable of being found with the stethoscope, called a "friction rub," a distinctive sound that can accompany diseases of the pericardium (the thin sac covering the surface of the heart), was also not recorded by his physicians. These negative findings may be important clues. That is, what was not detected by the stethoscope during his physicians' examinations may eliminate several possible causes for Chopin's failing health. However, just because Chopin's physicians couldn't detect an obvious heart murmur or friction rub on the basis of their exams doesn't mean the composer didn't have heart problems. Diagnosing certain forms of heart disease can be a tricky business, and this might be such an example. Chopin's heart was undoubtedly diseased at that point in his life, but determining the exact cause of the problem will need to be done retrospectively.

In August, Dr. Cruveilhier asked his two colleagues, Dr. Louis and Dr. Blache, to reexamine Chopin and offer their diagnostic help as well as any further advice they might have.[72] The three physicians, probably knowing the end was near and lacking any other diagnostic or therapeutic suggestions, could only recommend moving Chopin to a warmer apartment, preferably one with a sunnier exposure. Imagine hearing that double-edged advice from a contemporary physician. At this point, Stirling, now back in Paris and closely monitoring the details of Chopin's health, clandestinely arranged to provide the necessary funds to allow him to be moved into a spacious and bright apartment in the heart of one of the most prestigious addresses of the city, the fashionable Place Vendôme.

Laennec at the bedside.

Chopin chose to remain blissfully ignorant of his formerly dire financial situation and of the way the newly found money came to be in his account, a rather typical reaction of his to the details of his financial matters. He was delighted with the prospects for the change of quarters and took a keen interest in the luxurious apartment's decoration and furnishings in the days leading up to his move. Also buoying his spirits was the greatly anticipated arrival of his sister and her family later that month.

From the time she arrived, Ludwika remained by her brother's side day and night. His friends, still visiting despite the grim circumstances, noted that Chopin's legs were swollen and that his abdomen was distended. His color at times was dusky and, increasingly, he had greater difficulty breathing and speaking. Most likely his blood oxygen level was low, at times inadequate for clear thinking and alertness. Perhaps, too, his blood level of carbon dioxide became too high, either as a consequence of his cardiac or respiratory insufficiency. Weakness, lethargy, and irritability are all common symptoms of this condition. In the weeks immediately prior to his death, he also suffered bouts of extreme pain, although the existing accounts are not specific as to its character or location. The reports from his friends contend he endured his pain with tremendous courage and strength. Fortunately, morphine was used to combat his suffering.

The interior of Chopin's last apartment.

The frantically scribbled deathbed note, long ascribed to Chopin, has only recently been determined to have been written in 1844 by his father, Nicholas, during his own protracted death struggle.[73] Ironically, Nicholas Chopin had also suffered from a comparable form of respiratory insufficiency, generally assumed to have been also due to the ravages of tuberculosis. Sister, father, and now Chopin himself, each had been forced to contemplate the same hideous end. Choked and gasping for air, each panicked at the terrifying thought of being trapped inside an apparently lifeless body, mistakenly assumed to be bereft of life. The horror that Emilia never had time to express and that Chopin's father had sought to sidestep with his scrawled note to his doctor, the self-controlled composer took great pains to avert in his last request to Ludwika. After his death, Dr. Cruveilhier was to remove his heart, and his dear sister would bear it back to his beloved homeland. With a flourish befitting a great artist, Chopin had added the final barline to his life.

"*The Last Moments of Frédéric Chopin*" by Kwiatkowski.

Although Chopin's many biographers have unknowingly fashioned the falsely ascribed deathbed plea into a colorful climax to his long struggle with his fatal disease, myths need to be deconstructed and the truth served. Credit should be given to the dying Chopin for so presciently anticipating his fears of such an eventuality and for so carefully crafting his final preparations. His loved ones' tragic plight had taught him well.

In the early morning hours of October 17, his face darkened and his breathing became even more strained. Cruveilhier held a candle before Chopin's face and quietly asked him if he still was in pain. "No more" were his last words.

Later that same morning, the young Clésinger would arrive to fashion Chopin's plaster death mask and casts of the composer's hands. During much of the following year, he would labor assiduously to sculpt the lovely figure of Euterpe, known to the ancients as the muse of music, who now solemnly strums her silent lyre atop Chopin's tomb in Paris. A fellow Polish artist and well-known friend, Thèophile Kwiatkowski, who also had been present at the composer's last moments, would take the rest of the day to complete finely detailed drawings and a watercolor of the composer's profile.[74] Kwiatkowski had known Chopin ever since his own exile from Poland and resettlement in Paris in 1832, forced to leave his native country due to his intimate involvement in the failed Polish November Uprising of 1830 against the Russians. Over the many years of his friendship with Chopin, the artist would leave some forty-three portraits of his close friend, establishing himself as the most prolific and accurate recorder of the composer's distinctive features.

A watercolor/drawing of the composer shortly after his death.

Chopin's body would remain in his apartment through that entire day, presumably to allow a few others one final glimpse at their beloved friend. There was now only one last task to be completed before the composer's corpse would lie undisturbed in its casket. If Chopin's dying wish was to be honored, his heart would need to be removed. Would there be the unflinching resolve to proceed with this grisly undertaking?

As there was at this point no medical argument to cast doubt on Chopin's actual death, the only reason to remove the heart rested with Ludwika's desire to return her cherished brother's "soul" to Poland. However, Dr. Cruveilhier was obviously in no hurry to perform the absolutely token task of removing this now lifeless organ from a slowly cooling cadaver. He most likely had better things to do. It would not be until the third day after Chopin's death that Dr. Cruveilhier would find the time for this perfunctory postmortem courtesy. No doubt his heart wasn't in it! Considering his remarkably vague and ambivalent comments recorded during this procedure, he must not have given it his full attention. However cursory his effort, he did manage to place Chopin's heart in an alcohol-filled glass vessel and later handed it to Ludwika. Weeks later, she would conceal it carefully beneath her pleated skirts to avoid its discovery by the Russian guards at the Polish border as she determinedly returned her beloved brother's heart to his cherished homeland.

Frédéric Chopin's long struggle was over. For nearly half of his life he had struggled with the ravages of disease, fighting a chronic progressively debilitating illness that changed the course of his life. This illness, if indeed it were only a single entity, only accentuated his already melancholic disposition, thwarted his relationships with the loves of his life, and cut off his treasured ability to compose. Although some may disagree, most believe, as do I, that his wasting disease also influenced the character of his music. There remains little controversy, however, about the quality of Chopin's music or its ability to enthrall the many who hear it.

Chopin's now-lost death certificate, once completed by Dr. Cruveilhier, reportedly ascribed the cause of death to "tuberculosis of the lungs and larynx." However, in written correspondence with Stirling and Ludwika some months later, Cruveilhier expressed his doubts. In a letter Stirling wrote to Liszt, she quoted Cruveilhier as saying, "The autopsy did nothing to disclose the cause of death, but it appeared that the lungs were affected less than the heart. It is a disease I have never encountered before." Still later, Ludwika remembered Cruveilhier telling her that "the autopsy did nothing to disclose the cause of death...nevertheless he could not have survived... diverse pathology...enlarged heart...did not disclose pulmonary consumption...lung changes of many year (sic) duration...a disease not previously encountered."[75] The inconsistencies between the diagnosis documented in the death certificate and the subsequently reported correspondence are difficult to reconcile, unless one believes Cruveilhier, a most capable pathologic anatomist, came to reconsider his initial impressions. Yet Dr. Cruveilhier's hesitant and unclear observations hurriedly jotted down during that cursory task have formed the basis for the tuberculosis story for nearly two hundred years. These diagnostic incongruities, however puzzling, have also managed to perpetuate the controversy surrounding Chopin's illness and form the rationale for the search for a more suitable answer.

There is another possible explanation for Dr. Cruveilhier's ambivalent and mysteriously vague comments. He may only have been acceding to Ludwika's strong desire to protect her family's privacy. She may have asked him to suppress the gory pathologic observations he made of her dear brothers body.[76] After all, this was 1849, a time when it was not customary to allow public access to one's private medical matters. Autopsies were not then routinely performed, and especially not done to provide the gruesome details of a person's death just to satisfy unending public curiosity. For Ludwika, her brother's heart was her private concern. It certainly was not a matter for public debate and analysis. Besides, she must then have been greatly preoccupied with just how she was going to get this treasured item all the way back to Poland. Perhaps she now wished to divert the focus of attention of Chopin's many admirers toward a reflection on his musical legacy and away from any discreet medical mysteries concerning his final illness. Her possible collusion with Dr. Cruveilhier may simply have been a deliberate attempt to protect her brother's growing reputation. Whether purposely obscure or merely sloppy, Dr. Cruveilhier's confusing report still elicits much current interest as its equivocation prompts some interesting and intriguing diagnostic options.

Following His Heart

"One learns people through the heart,
not the eyes or the intellect."
Mark Twain

Before proceeding with a detailed review of the numerous candidates for the cause of Chopin's demise, I think it first would
be fitting to follow the peripatetic path of his poor heart. It's a story
in itself and one filled with many unforeseen developments, some of
which may still be unwritten. Although this unfamiliar account may
comparatively only shed faint light on the primary subject of our investigation, its telling nevertheless adds much to the ongoing mystery
of this man's genius and his continuing influence in the world. Chopin
certainly changed the course of Classical music, but now can his heart
also have an influence on the course of scientific discovery? His heart's
long journey may not yet be over if one considers that the compelling
quest for certainty and the current proposal to reopen its sealed crystal
enclosure may together lead the way to an altogether new stratum of
scrutiny and significance for current scientific investigation.

According to Chopin's nephew, his eldest sister Ludwika's son,
Anthony Jedrzejewicz, his mother would often relate to him the story
that, in his final hours, Frédéric Chopin had pleaded with her to take
his heart back to Poland, saying that while he knew the authorities
would never allow the return of his body, "…take at least my heart."[77]
Dutifully, like the responsible oldest sibling she always was, Ludwika
would comply with her beloved brother's request, yet her journey back

to Poland wouldn't be without its own perils and intrigue. Despite adversity, love usually finds a way.

Once safely back in Warsaw and still uncertain where her brother's heart would eventually rest, she decided to keep the urn in her family's home. By that time her aged mother was its sole occupant, as her father had died many years earlier. This location would prove to be a wise choice, for Ludwika would die rather quickly and unexpectedly of an unidentified respiratory disorder during the plague epidemic of 1855. After Chopin's mother's death in 1861, it was then left to the sole surviving sibling, Izabella, to look after the cherished vessel. By this time, Chopin's heart had already surreptitiously passed through several countries and, more openly, through many loving hands, yet there would still be more journeys to come. Some of those hands would not be nearly as kindhearted.

In her final years, Izabella herself would search for a suitable resting place for her brother's heart. Accordingly, she began her quest by inquiring at her family's local parish church, the Holy Cross Church in Warsaw. Initially, however, the religious authorities resisted her request, claiming that only saints could be interred within the crypts of the church. The priests readily acknowledged the quality of Chopin's wonderfully expressive works and easily accepted him as a great musical genius but, after recollecting his widely publicized illicit affair with the colorful and controversial George Sand, in no way could they consider him a saint! Eventually, a compromise was struck: his heart wouldn't be buried in the crypts, but rather in a *column* in the revered church. There were already a few other notables who had found their ultimate repose in that esteemed temple, yet they too had been buried *above* the floor, safely above the holy crypts and catacombs where the more saintly souls so solemnly lay. Izabella was greatly relieved to secure what she felt was the perfect final resting spot for her brother's heart, a place she felt satisfied her brother and her entire family would have admired.

On March 1, 1879, the anniversary of Chopin's birth in 1810 and some thirty years after his death, his heart was quietly entombed in the first pillar on the left in the Church of the Holy Cross. The simple ceremony took place in the evening, without fanfare, without noise or music, in a darkening sanctuary and in the presence of only a few people. His heart had already traveled more than a thousand miles from its master's chest since his untimely death many years earlier.

To those witnessing the heart's quiet and dignified interment, it must have seemed like ages since Chopin's body had been buried in the Père Lachaise Cemetery in Paris. Certainly, they accepted this would be the appropriate end to his heart's long journey, a satisfactory conclusion to Frédéric Chopin's existence and influence. Why would there be any doubt?

In September of 1939, the first bombs of the German invasion exploded throughout Warsaw. Chopin's heart, which until now had only heard the sounds of the church's magnificent organ, countless religious hymns, and the soft murmuring of many prayers, suddenly awoke to the shocking screams of war. The bombing of the Blitzkrieg would continue relentlessly without mercy until, as had been so presciently predicted by the Führer, it was rapidly followed by Poland's abject defeat. Then came the oppressive reality of foreign occupation. The Nazis, no strangers to the immense importance of the Catholic Church in Poland, quickly assumed control of the Holy Cross Church and brazenly used it as a headquarters to conduct their wartime activities. Knowing its enormous significance to the strength of the Polish spirit, the clever Nazis soon announced that Chopin's music would henceforth be banned from performance or broadcast throughout the country. Imagine, a person could be killed for playing the music of Chopin! The very lifeblood of Poland that for so many years had helped sustain its indomitable essence and patriotism—the stirring chords of Chopin's *Polonaise, Op. 53,* the reflective strains of his *Ballade No. 4,* and the soothing melancholy of his many nocturnes—were to be heard no more. His music had come to a full stop.

By August of 1944, the Polish Resistance Movement in Warsaw had gained sufficient strength to launch a significant counteroffensive, later to be called the Warsaw Uprising. These dedicated Polish insurgents managed many small guerilla-style successes, one of them being the retaking of their venerated Holy Cross Church on August 23. The resourceful Poles even made sure there would be a Polish film crew on hand to record the success of their battle. However, the exhausted and poorly equipped insurgents failed to retain the church and its complex of buildings after the Germans launched a series of fierce attacks that ultimately drove them out and seriously destroyed large parts of the edifice. There are grisly reports of the determined Resistance fighters still shooting from the dark recesses of the choir loft as the Germans ruthlessly ripped out the treasured old organ pipes to get at them. A quickly prepared insurgent newsletter gravely reported to a stunned nation that the "church façade and towers were completely destroyed. For Warsaw it is a painful loss in the church where Chopin's heart was kept."[78] The loss of Chopin's heart was the loss of an inestimably important cultural treasure, a major tragedy for the proud Polish nation. People were in a state of shock. Had his heart finally come to the end of its long journey?

Realizing what a devastating blow this sad news was to their concerned countrymen, the Resistance within days broadcast the stunning announcement from its underground radio station that Chopin's heart actually had not been destroyed, but in fact was still in the safe hands of the Polish Army Office of Information and Propaganda, at the time led by a Lieutenant Moczarski. This hapless fellow, rushed and desperate to downplay the terrible news of this disaster, was only doing what he knew best in coming up with what was so obviously a fabricated piece of Polish propaganda. The plucky lieutenant kept publicly denying this unpalatable misfortune even though he was painfully aware that the Nazis already had Chopin's heart firmly in their grasp.

What happened to the heart? How did it wind up so quickly in German possession? Was it indeed damaged or destroyed? The explanation involves another of those odd twists of fate so common in this Chopin story, one that serves to demonstrate once again the alluring power of Chopin's music to deny conventional logic and rationale, even during the uncertain course of a deadly war.

The following strange chain of events would be witnessed by the Reverend Charles Mrowiec, the head priest of the Holy Cross Church from 1943 to 1960. Immediately before the final battle for the church and before it was largely destroyed, Mrowiec had been secretly approached by a German Army chaplain by the name of Schultze (or Schulze). Schultze knew of the importance of this relic to the Polish people and, for that matter, to humanity, and so offered to remove and protect the heart from its certain harm during the impending hostilities. He also promised to return it when things calmed down. He did this without authorization from anyone; he was acting solely on his own and based on his own considerable admiration for the Polish composer. He must have been a pragmatist and a realist, irrespective of his religious trappings. Having essentially no other options and seeing no other way of keeping their revered relic safe, Mrowiec and his fellow priests reluctantly acquiesced to Schultze's unusual request.

Trusting the enemy with their country's most cherished cultural treasure was not something these panicked priests could easily swallow, and it certainly must attest to the strength of this Nazi chaplain's personality and impressive powers of persuasion. Straightway, Schultze and a few other German soldiers carefully removed the urn from its already cracked column and quickly vanished into the blackness of the Warsaw night. Chopin's heart was on the move once again!

Rather unexpectedly, the next narrative of our story comes from a former Nazi General in the SS Division, a certain Heinz Reinefarth. A notoriously ruthless Nazi officer, by his actions he was responsible for countless thousands of Polish deaths, a gruesome legacy of despicable carnage that included several mass murders. Reinefarth's unalloyed toughness must later have been tempered by practical expediency, however, as at the end of war he was furiously accused of not adequately defending his position "to the last man" by none other than an incensed Adolf Hitler. This widely remembered Nazi general continues to be reviled throughout Poland for his shockingly insensitive statement, "We have more prisoners than ammunition to kill them."[79] Far luckier than his commanding officer, the equally infamous General Erich von dem Bach, Reinefarth somehow evaded war crimes prosecution and imprisonment to live rather too comfortably on his generous retirement pension until his death in 1979.

In his recollections some thirty years after the end of WWII, Reinefarth remembered a peculiar episode that occurred while he was stationed in Warsaw. He reported that he had been confined to his quarters suffering from an acute and quite miserable attack of dysentery when suddenly an officer entered his room and promptly placed a compact and rather heavy leather case at the foot of his sickbed, claiming that it was a religious relic of some sort. After carefully inspecting it and finding some letters of a name on its outer case, Reinefarth quickly took to the strange back channels of wartime communication, eventually reaching the Archbishop of Warsaw, who was hidden far from the dangers of the city, to ask him about this supposed relic. As the name the general mentioned turned out to be no saint ever known to the archbishop, it remained for a few more awkward minutes a continued mystery (the name Reinefarth had given was later traced to the manufacturer of the box itself). Probing further and uncovering an ebony box with an ornate heart-shaped silver plaque on its top, Reinefarth suddenly saw the engraved name of Chopin, complete with his dates of birth and death, and immediately realized what he had in his hands.[80] The powerful and crafty Nazi would not for the moment be willing to disclose to the puzzled archbishop just what it was he had in his possession, wishing to gain time to explore the interesting possibilities this intriguing box, this newly acquired treasure, might have to offer.

The general would eventually describe an elegant ebony box closely enclosing yet another box, this second one of oak, that itself contained a hermetically sealed glass container. Reinefarth quickly comprehended he held a powerful propaganda tool he might use to quiet the incensed and agitated Poles. Almost immediately, he saw the political wisdom of returning the cherished heart to the Polish church hierarchy in a grand public gesture of Nazi "brotherhood." Accordingly, in a well-orchestrated and very conspicuous ceremony, complete with a German propaganda film crew, military band, and full color guard, Chopin's heart would be marched through the heart of a bomb-damaged Warsaw by a large contingent of Nazi soldiers on September 9, 1944. Certainly, this must have been the only military march in which Chopin ever participated!

Ironically, *Kaplan* Schultze, the foresighted pragmatist who most certainly saved Chopin's heart from desecration and destruction, would not survive the war himself. He would perish in the Soviet offensive of 1945 and remains unidentified to this day. With a name like Schultze, so common among Germans and Austrians, there has been no way to ferret out the details of his life, nor pay tribute to his judicious deed. Whether he truly believed that Chopin's heart would ever be returned to its sanctuary in Poland is anyone's guess. The fact that the relic quickly found its way into the hands of the shrewd General Reinefarth, however, makes any overly flattering judgment of this chaplain's character rather indecorous for its clandestine rescuer. To be kind, perhaps Chaplain Schultze might be praised for his audacity and forgiven for his moral ambivalence, likened to some Shakespearean pawn caught up in a complicated plot twist and unaware of his drama's overall design.

Chopin's heart, with Nazi cameras rolling and a spirited military band playing, was soon ceremoniously presented to the Archbishop of Warsaw. He in turn would place it on top of a piano in the chapel of his rectory, where it would remain unmolested until October 17, 1945, the ninety-sixth anniversary of the composer's death. On that day, a Father Leopold Petrzyk, a new pastor of the Holy Cross Church, and a Professor Woytowicz would arrive at the rectory to take the heart to Chopin's birthplace, the nearby estate at Żelazowa Wola. Accompanying them on their journey was a quiet Polish man by the name of Bronisław Edward Sydow. There will more to tell about him later.

Chopin's heart had now come full circle. It had returned to its origins in the beloved home of his youth. It had powered the marvelous skills of a creative musical genius while laboring for years under the restrictions of an unknown chronic illness. It had defeated the best diagnostic capabilities of the leading medical authorities in France, disclosing nothing of its troubles despite the incessant probing of the best physicians of the time and their latest medical invention, the stethoscope. It had survived the threat of capture by the occupying Russian authorities after having been carefully hidden beneath the thick skirts of a matronly middle-aged woman. It had survived wartime destruction by two armies during separate military assaults on its resting place in the Holy Cross Church. It had been used as a potent propaganda tool by an occupying foreign army and had then been paraded through the ruined streets of Warsaw, past thousands of flag-waving admirers uneasily trying to celebrate during an oppressive occupation. It was back home now. Could it finally rest in this tranquil setting of peace and quiet?

Bronisław Sydow must have been an interesting fellow. Raised in Poland, for unknown reasons he decided to pursue his formal training at the University of Chile, the largest and oldest institution of public learning in that country, and still one of the most prestigious schools in South America. Although he would eventually become a leading Polish musicologist, his degree was in economics, not music. Sydow is now recognized for his important contributions to the compilation of a complete and accurate bibliography of Chopin, and had made it his special project to record and document as many of the various letters of the composer as he could find. He would later publish multiple articles about Chopin, even once documenting his observations of the preserved heart for the Polish Chopin Society, but first he would have to return to Poland. What lured him back to his homeland remains a mystery. What convinced him to devote much of his life to gathering Chopin's correspondence is another. And exactly why Sydow would find himself in the backseat of an automobile carrying Chopin's heart back to its humble origins just adds to the puzzle. Perhaps it was his proximity to this honored object that stirred his already strong passions for the composer. If indeed it were, he would only be one of many who would be changed by his contact with that well-traveled vestige of Chopin.

In 1951, the heart would be returned to Warsaw for its interment into its prior resting place in the now-rebuilt and painstakingly restored Church of the Holy Cross. This time it would be carried by none other than Bronisław Sydow, now established as a respected musicologist with a particular bent for the music and correspondence of Frédéric Chopin. The great confidence the leading authorities had in this man was displayed in their giving him the exclusive task of opening the boxes containing the heart, removing the crystal urn, and describing for the world what he saw. Sydow had not been trained as a medical doctor or even as a scientist. Why he was chosen for this task instead of a qualified pathologist or forensic expert must forever remain a disturbing riddle, and it speaks to the ignorance of those entrusted with one of the historic opportunities of a lifetime. It wasn't the first bumbling with Chopin's precious heart, yet would it be the last?

A Polish newsreel still of Chopin's heart being returned to Warsaw.

Sydow did his best at describing what he saw and at least included a few clues to whet the interest of today's medical researchers. His detailed examination, although severely compromised by his medically untrained capabilities, was written in a report submitted to the Warsaw Chopin Society in October of 1951, at about the same time the heart was reinterred. He corrected the German general's account of the boxes, claiming that the outer box was made from oak, the inner of mahogany (the report would later be changed to read "ebony"), and he described the beautiful silver heart-shaped plaque that had been fashioned into a clasp on the top of the inner box. "Inside this box is a crystal jar, hermetically-sealed, in which the clear spirit is the well-preserved heart of Chopin. Conspicuous is the size of the heart; for a figure of average height, it is exceeding large."[81]

There are so many other observations that he could have made. Just knowing a few of them would go a long way toward settling the present controversy about the disease Chopin suffered. Sydow's honest attempts at a medical description of a bodily organ entirely new to his experience as an economy student and musicologist fall far short of any forensic adequacy for a meaningful postmortem analysis. Admittedly, it's difficult to judge Sydow too harshly, as his complete report has been kept in private hands with very specific instructions to its keepers to not divulge any more than that which is already in the public record. Recently, I have obtained a copy of the full report and have reexamined it occasionally as I have attempted to diagnose Chopin's disease.

Chopin's heart was indeed large and, by carefully reconstructing the evidence gleaned from the currently available historical files, we learn that he did apparently succumb to a type of congestive heart failure. Would releasing Sydow's suppressed report clarify the matter? Is another attempt at a pathologic description of the heart something that is desired? Perhaps future investigators, made fully cognizant of the clumsy missteps of the past, will be able to fashion a forensic analysis so scientifically complete and yet so unobtrusive in its approach that any public display of disruption to this revered relic will be minimal and unnoticed. Or conversely, these same historical blunders might only serve to restrain those now responsible for the heart's preservation from granting *any* future access. Will his heart forever be destined to rest in the dark enclosure of its marble sanctuary, never to be scrutinized by much more knowledgeable eyes?

The Holy Cross Church in Warsaw.

Chopin's heart would eventually make its way back into the Holy Cross Church, this time in a procession not accompanied by the harsh strains of military music but rather by the majestically solemn refrain from the third movement of his *Piano Sonata in B flat minor, Op. 35*. Special care would be taken to replace the carved plaque overlaying the crypt, with the fervent hope from all those present that this esteemed treasure of Poland would never again be removed from this shrine to his genius. Undoubtedly, there were a few sage souls among those in attendance at that ceremony who resigned themselves to accept the reality that there are no guarantees in this world. Yet, even they would not have been able to foresee that this hallowed shrine would once again be under siege nearly sixty years later.

Now that we know the story of what has happened to Chopin's heart during all these years, it's time to return to our quest to identify the illness that sickened and killed Frédéric Chopin. When exactly did it start and how did it cause his death? Are there additional clues to its diagnosis? It's time to examine the many possibilities more closely in search for an answer.

Debating the Possibilities

"Dying is a very dull, dreary affair. And my advice to you
is to have nothing whatever to do with it."
W. Somerset Maugham

During the past quarter of a century, there have been several comprehensive reviews, largely in the medical literature, addressing the topic of Chopin's illness. The worldwide undiminished popularity of the great Polish composer's music, still widely performed two hundred years after his birth, undoubtedly is a major reason for the ongoing interest in his life. Yet it has been the rapid scientific advance in our understanding of several illnesses that have really fueled this more detailed inquiry into the cause of his protracted illness and early death at the age of thirty-nine.

Most of these articles postulate that Chopin did not die from pulmonary tuberculosis, as has been commonly believed. The tuberculosis theory was debated even while he lived yet, in the absence of any reasonable alternative explanation, it has long been presumed to be the cause of Chopin's chronic suffering and eventual death. In fact, it has become nearly a legend, perpetuated rather unknowingly by his many biographers as well as his adoring public. The leading hypothesis in most of these recent medical reviews postulates that Chopin was afflicted with the complex heritable disease cystic fibrosis. Also contributing to this controversy has been the fairly recent and rather astonishing medical discovery that cystic fibrosis, long considered only a disease of children, can have its onset in adulthood.[82] Advances in the understanding of genetics have demonstrated the tremendous variability of this disease and help to explain the multiple possible manifestations of its clinical course. It's now recognized that milder forms of cystic fibrosis can and do exist in adults, often revealing themselves through a rather insidious array of symptoms.[83,84] Armed with the latest scientific knowledge of this multifarious disease, physicians are now able to diagnose it with greater accuracy and in a wider range of patients. Intriguingly, some of these scientists, especially those with an interest in Chopin, have also sought to use this new information to look retrospectively. Their curiosity of the medical mysteries of the past and their desire to untangle the diagnostic dilemma in the complicated case of Chopin's illness now drive their research efforts.

Some of the recent scientific discoveries have proven helpful to current sufferers afflicted with cystic fibrosis, but can this information also be used to identify and diagnose what happened to those long dead? The answer is a qualified yes. The genetic basis of cystic fibrosis, as traced through the complicated patterns of DNA, permits a reflective look at the lives of those deceased, a particularly useful inquiry for those who may not have been accurately diagnosed during their lifetimes. If scientists have been able to discover the genetic secrets gathered from the ancient remains of dinosaurs and Egyptian pharaohs, can't they also solve the medical mysteries of those dying in the more recent past, such as, for example, in our analysis, two hundred years ago? Well, it depends on a lot of things. For example, the tissues selected for any DNA analysis must be of a sufficiently decent quality to provide reasonable answers. Then the genetic patterns found must be considered to be acceptably specific for the disease in question. That is, for it to be helpful, the DNA evidence must point to the realistic probabilities for that disease and not just its theorized possibilities.[85] Science is often complicated, and this is a good example. Before going into more details about cystic fibrosis and how it might have been the illness that sickened Chopin, however, it's necessary to lay out some basic information about the other diagnostic considerations.

Despite the recent flurry in interest in cystic fibrosis, tuberculosis still must remain a leading candidate. Tuberculosis was a very common cause of illness and death in Chopin's day. It was widely known to attack those most susceptible, the weak and undernourished. Is that why he may have acquired this disease? Chopin certainly was never recognized for his physical strength or stamina, or for having an especially ravenous appetite. Never weighing more than one hundred pounds, even in his prime, he appeared small and poorly nourished to those who knew him best, especially his parents. And furthermore, he was literally surrounded by the disease. If one believes tuberculosis was responsible for the deaths of his younger sister, Emilia, his close friends Jan Białobłocki and Jan Matuszyński, his pupil Karl Filtsch, and perhaps even his father, then it may be easier to assume Chopin also shared this common infection. The fact that his older sister, Ludwika, died in her late forties of an undefined respiratory ailment also may add weight to the argument for tuberculosis. Interestingly, recent scientific investigations have revealed a genetic link for this disease.[86] It's now known that persons lacking particular genes are more susceptible to tuberculosis, confirming what some scientists have hypothesized for many years. Could Chopin's entire family have been genetically more susceptible to this disease?

Most of Chopin's physicians, and there were many during his life-time, believed he was consumptive. Only a few expressed their doubt, and then their reasons for any diagnostic uncertainty were never spelled out. Chopin's first documented significant illness, the episode of glandular swelling in his neck accompanied by his prolonged fatigue and debility, could fit with an initial infection with the tubercle bacillus, although we now know that most of the primary infections with this disease are silent and devoid of symptomatology. The vast majority of individuals initially infected with the tubercle bacillus, *Mycobacterium tuberculosis,* do not display the protracted course of symptoms the adolescent Chopin suffered when he was sixteen. However, his persistent coughing of blood-streaked sputum that began in his twenties is a classic harbinger of tuberculosis. To the many who attended his concerts, he certainly looked like a consumptive: he appeared pale, underweight, and coughed continually. Their accounts were based on their personal firsthand observations after witnessing this very prevalent disease in their communities yet, to be fair for purposes of argument, the appearance of a person with tuberculosis might be identical to that of a person with cystic fibrosis, or for that matter, to that of many other ailments. Appearances are sometimes deceiving.

Then there is the telling argument that it would be most unlikely for an individual with untreated tuberculosis to survive nearly twenty-four years with this disease. It's no doubt possible, but usually much more likely to last this long in those stronger individuals who enjoy better overall health. From all reports, Chopin did not enjoy a robust physical constitution and his often-peculiar food preferences and sedentary lifestyle probably did little to preserve his strength. It could be theorized that his adolescent illness was not tuberculosis; presumably, it was a condition more resembling mononucleosis but, as his blood-tinged coughing episodes began when he was twenty, that would still postulate that tuberculosis was accountable for nearly two decades of illness! In addition, if one maintains Chopin may have had an inherent genetic susceptibility to tuberculosis, then his decades-long struggle with this disease appears even more suspect.

There is also the need to reexamine the somewhat bizarre account of Dr. Cruveilhier. His complete autopsy report, forever lost to the flames of history, must certainly be considered a critical missing link, a key to unraveling this medical mystery. Despite Cruveilhier's straightforward attestation of tuberculosis on Chopin's death certificate, his rambling and fragmentary thoughts subsequently recorded in the secondhand accounts of Stirling and Ludwika only serve to increase our uncertainty as to the accuracy of his initial impression. Why would Jean Baptiste Cruveilhier, the leading expert in his day on pathological anatomy, and perhaps the foremost authority on tuberculosis in all of France, choose to express his diagnostic doubts only in his private correspondence after Chopin's death? These vacillations cannot be construed as mere idle musings for one so well trained as he. But was he really that much of an expert?

Astonishingly, Dr. Cruveilhier was not as highly regarded for his clinical skills as a practicing physician as he was for his acumen in the field of anatomical study.[87] Most of his patients were already cadavers by the time he saw them, and not living, breathing organisms with mysterious symptoms to fathom or noisy chest cavities to auscultate with a crude stethoscope. His reputation had been primarily established for his skills as an anatomic researcher and not those of a practicing physician. The fact that Cruveilhier had once catered to the royals probably influenced the always class-conscious Chopin in his selection of this practitioner more than any real regard for his clinical abilities. Matters of style and bearing were always important to Chopin. Having practiced for decades, I'm convinced patients often make poor decisions choosing their physicians and do exactly what Chopin did!

Jean Baptiste Cruveilhier, Chopin's last physician.

Other inconsistencies turn our attention away from tuberculosis. The digestive complaints that pop up occasionally in Chopin's biographies are not well explained by tuberculosis and may fit better with the multi-organ disease of cystic fibrosis. The vast majority (up to 90 percent) of patients with cystic fibrosis, and especially those with the adult form of the disease, suffer from problems with the liver and pancreas, organs essential for digestion. Disease in these organs commonly leads to digestive symptoms and diarrhea, something Chopin was reported to suffer either frequently or occasionally, depending on which historical accounts one chooses to believe. Liver disease also can cause a buildup of fluid in the abdominal cavity, something witnessed by many observers in the last weeks of Chopin's life. Although his abdominal swelling may have been linked to cystic fibrosis, it might also have been the manifestation of heart failure. Any severe disease of the lungs can be linked to heart failure, a complex set of physical problems that reflect the diminished capacity of the heart muscle to do its job. With lung disease especially, the right, or "filling," side of the heart is involved first, leading to heart failure's main symptom of breathlessness with exertion, and the physical findings of leg swelling and abdominal distention. Most of the medical reviews postulate Chopin had heart failure; they disagree on what caused it.

The famous French author and Chopin's acquaintance, Honoré de Balzac, died from complications of heart failure in 1850.[88] During the decade before his death, his physicians correctly determined he suffered from valvular damage to his heart. For years he had experienced breathlessness and difficulty walking uphill. We now can speculate that he had a classic case of *rheumatic heart disease* with valvular damage to his heart, undoubtedly caused by his repeated exposure to the streptococcal bacterium. How were his doctors able to know this? After all, there were no electrocardiograms, echocardiograms, or chest x-ray machines available to these pioneering medical practitioners. They were able to identify his heart disease by using Laennec's newly introduced stethoscope. Crude as it was, little more than a hollowed out piece of wood, this rudimentary device allowed his doctors to detect the characteristic sounds of a heart weakened by valves no longer able to provide the necessary dynamics essential to its function of pumping blood through the body.

Balzac's physicians practiced in the very same hospitals as the doctors who looked after Chopin. Had Chopin suffered from a similar form of valvular heart disease, his astute physicians would have recognized it immediately. The *absence* of abnormal sounds during their repeated examinations of Chopin's lungs and heart only confused them rather than added any useful information to their diagnostic views. The additional features of Chopin's symptoms, including his fevers, chills, sinus congestion, and coughing, do not fit the picture of valvular heart disease. Rheumatic fever accompanied by significant heart valve damage is also unlikely to develop during one's adolescent years, usually taking many decades to inflict its damage, and is equally improbable to persist for twenty or more years after causing pulmonary hemorrhage. Therefore, the theory that Chopin suffered an episode of rheumatic fever when he was sixteen and then only a few years later developed its associated valvular incompetency appears weak. Valvular heart disease was not the illness that befell Chopin. If he had heart disease, it was of a different kind.

Some medical researchers have considered that Chopin suffered from a disease of his immune system.[89] They point to the fact that he suffered repeated infections year after year, and had apparent great difficulty in recovering from them, often suffering protracted periods of debility. The general medical term for this condition is *hypogammaglobulinemia*, a tongue-twister of a name indicating a deficiency in the level of immunoglobulins, those blood-borne proteins in our bodies that enable us to fight infection effectively. It, too, is a genetically transmitted disease, but its pattern of illness just does not fit that of Chopin's disease. A person with this disorder is subject to repeated infections not only in the respiratory tract, the primary location of Chopin's problems, but almost everywhere else and especially in the skin. The lack of this pattern in Chopin's youth and the absence of any known serious infections beyond his respiratory tract clearly eliminate this diagnosis as well.

Another proposed candidate for Chopin's illness has been an unusual form of *emphysema*.[90] Today known better by its acronym, COPD (chronic obstructive pulmonary disease), emphysema is a disease usually associated with heavy smoking. To the best of our knowledge, Chopin did not smoke, and it's very doubtful his relatively brief exposure to the secondhand puffs from George Sand's occasional smelly cigar could really be held responsible for his illness. Besides, Chopin was suffering with his symptoms long before he met Sand, being ill before he was twenty, something distinctly unusual for a disease characteristically linked to decades of tobacco exposure.

Yet there is another form of emphysema, one not nearly as well known, not linked to smoking, and—most significantly for the purposes of the Chopin investigation—with its onset in adolescence. It, too, is a genetic disorder that leads to a deficiency of a critical protein necessary to maintain the elasticity of the lungs. Other critical body functions are also affected, with most suffering from progressive pancreatic and liver disease. Without this crucial chemical, the progressive breakdown of lung tissue occurs, leading to the symptoms of breathlessness, frequent infections, coughing, and eventually an early death. The multi-organ nature of this disease means that those afflicted will also suffer weight loss, weakness, and digestive disturbances. Its name is another mouthful, *alpha 1-antitrypsin deficiency*, and, despite not being a particularly familiar term, it's not that uncommon a disease. The most serious form of this genetic ailment can occur in one out every one thousand individuals, with milder forms of the disease occurring in as many as 4 percent of the population. For unknown reasons, it has been found to be more common in the peoples of northern Europe.[91]

If one accepts that alpha 1-antitrypsin deficiency affected the Chopin family, it could explain Emilia's early death. She died at fourteen after a massive episode of bleeding, either from her lungs or upper digestive tract. Her hemorrhage was so sudden and substantial that it did not allow precise localization of its source, but it could have been from a condition known as *portal hypertension*, a complication from the liver disease associated with this genetic deficiency. On the other hand, she may have died from a tubercular infection that had invaded into the blood vessels of her bronchial tubes, with a similar disastrous demise. The digestive difficulties present in those with the deficiency of this antitrypsin also leave most victims with chronic diarrhea. Although this complaint occasionally runs through the story of our composer's life, it does not seem to appear with the sufficient frequency necessary to make the alpha 1-antitrypsin diagnosis highly compelling. Also, if one analyzes the Chopin family tree, going through his mother's and his father's relatives in both directions, there is only one death that could be considered premature in eight generations.[92] That is, looking back over the several generations of relatives who lived prior to his parents, together with a review of the lives of those many generations of relatives linked to Ludwika, his only sibling with children, does not disclose the pattern that might be expected with this genetic disorder. Although certainly reasonable, the choice of alpha 1-antitrypsin deficiency would appear to be less plausible.

There are other diagnostic possibilities to consider, although admittedly, they too must be viewed as most unlikely. I've added them to the list because they share some common features with the clinical course shown by Chopin over his brief life. No amount of argument or speculation can be expected to add further support for or diminish the likelihood of any of these rare diseases being established as the cause of his illness. I am merely including them for the sake of completeness. Even if there were to be a careful scientific analysis conducted on the extant remains of the Polish composer, it's doubtful with current knowledge that it would be possible to determine whether any of these conditions had ever been present.

With this caveat in mind, an additional possibility includes *bronchopulmonary aspergillosis*, a type of allergic respiratory reaction to a common soil fungus.[93] It could possibly explain the seasonal variation Chopin himself observed in his symptoms, but its requirement of pre-existing allergies and asthma all accompanied by the predominant symptom of loud wheezing, something not present in the Chopin story, strongly argues against its inclusion.

The next possible diagnosis is that of a chronic *lung abscess*, continually spilling its purulent contents over into Chopin's bronchial tubes and being responsible for the episodic hemorrhagic coughing. The decades-long course of his illness, however, dictates against this choice.

A condition called *bronchiectasis* certainly must be considered. Granted, most medical scholars believe that Chopin indeed had this problem, but it's usually a secondary problem. That is, bronchiectasis, or the progressive dilatation and thickening of the bronchial tubes, is often caused by another illness. Both tuberculosis and cystic fibrosis, for example, can cause this condition. As a primary cause of Chopin's long decline and death, bronchiectasis alone appears unlikely.

A very rare disease, *Churg-Strauss syndrome*, has also been mentioned as a possibility. An odd combination of allergic asthma and an immune-mediated inflammation of blood vessels throughout the body, it too seems improbable to have been the disease that affected Chopin.

There is one more important piece to this puzzle that has not been previously discussed. It concerns a rather obscure physical finding, an anatomical abnormality of the fingertips that physicians notice in their patients who suffer from some forms of severe lung disease. It also accompanies some forms of cancer, especially cancer of the lung. It can also occur in *cirrhosis* of the liver, a condition Chopin was not thought to suffer. The finding is called clubbing, and its complete absence in Chopin's case is an important clue to the identity of his disease. This strange condition, characterized by the easily recognized bulbous enlargement of the fingertips, occurs when the lungs are unable to supply adequate oxygen to the ends of the circulatory tree. There are other more mysterious factors at work here, too, most likely genetic, that contribute to this physical phenomenon. It's sufficient to say that clubbing is a well-recognized manifestation of cystic fibrosis. In fact, it's so common in this disease, especially if its course is of long duration, that the absence of this phenomenon is strong evidence against its diagnosis.[94] Clubbing does occur in cases of pulmonary tuberculosis, but to a much lesser extent than with cystic fibrosis.

It has already been mentioned that Chopin's son-in-law, Jean-Baptiste Auguste Clésinger, took plaster casts of Chopin's hands only hours after the composer's death.[95] These original casts still exist, with thousands of copies now distributed over the globe. I have one beside me on my desk as I write this. These reproductions of the pianist's hands do not display any evidence of clubbing.[96] There is no debate on this. As if there were not already enough challenges in establishing Chopin's diagnosis by means of a postmortem analysis, the absence of this important physical finding may present even more obstacles to our identification of his disease.

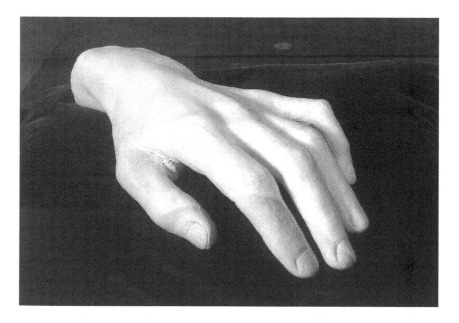

Plaster cast of Chopin's hand.

What, then, are we left to consider? Of the many possible diseases that might have so changed Chopin's life, which now remain the likely candidates for our analysis? With our present medical knowledge, the two leading diagnostic aspirants must be either cystic fibrosis or tuberculosis. The possibility of an alpha 1-antitrypsin deficiency still exists, but I believe this diagnosis is less tenable. I maintain that it's presently impossible to take this investigation to the point of certainty without the ability to conduct further pathological and DNA analyses on the remains of Chopin. Obviously this weighty requirement presents formidable challenges, with countless political, cultural, ethical, religious, and personal issues to be considered, each a considerable barrier to such an intrusive investigation.

In 2008, the Polish Minister of Culture, Bogdan Zdrojewski, and the director of the highly esteemed Fryderyk Chopin Institute in Warsaw, Grzegorz Michalski, received a detailed request for a DNA analysis of Chopin's heart. This scientific inquiry had been proposed by a leading Polish cystic fibrosis expert, Professor Wojciech Cichy. Cichy was then a sixty-six-year-old Professor of Pediatrics and Chair of Pediatric Gastroenterology and Metabolic Diseases at the Medical University in Poznan. With more than forty years of experience in working with cystic fibrosis patients, Cichy is an internationally recognized researcher in the field. He is the leading medical advisor to the Matio Foundation, a Polish organization assisting the victims of cystic fibrosis. He also had managed to assemble an impressive team of scientific investigators, each skilled in the latest techniques of DNA analysis, who were to join him in this inquiry. If anybody could accomplish the challenging task of determining whether Chopin suffered from cystic fibrosis, Professor Cichy and his capable team certainly met all the necessary prerequisites for a successful effort.

How had this seasoned Polish physician become so intrigued by Chopin's illness? It certainly wasn't that he didn't have enough to do. It was clearly apparent to all who knew Cichy that he was already heavily burdened while serving in his multiple capacities, clinical and administrative. So why would he now wish to assume the added responsibility for what he must have known would become an enormously controversial challenge with a distinctly international compass? A review of the Professor's long record of distinguished accomplishments and life experiences quickly provides the impression of a man who enjoys a vigorous challenge and a diversity of experience. Perhaps of even greater significance was Cichy's Polish heritage, with its culturally endowed overarching interest in all things Chopin. He appeared to possess all the necessary personal and professional attributes for the complex task at hand. Fortunately, he also held in his heart the passion to proceed.

Professor Cichy has since recounted for me the story how he happened to come across an old text about Chopin, a book written at the turn of the last century by the famous Polish writer and historian Ferdynand Hoesick. In his exhaustive three-volume summary of Chopin's life and works, Hoesick provided a detailed description of Chopin's symptoms. He had garnered these descriptions from a careful review of old records, letters, and the then-available literature.

Cichy told me he was immediately struck by the similarity of Chopin's symptoms to those of his cystic fibrosis patients. He quickly theorized that the beloved Polish composer could likely have suffered from this dreadful disease he knew all too well. Then and there, he vowed to continue searching for an answer.

Doing his own literature search, Cichy then ran across Dr. O'Shea's article in *The Medical Journal of Australia* claiming cystic fibrosis provided the best explanation for the disease suffered by Chopin. Armed with his own extensive personal experience and this additional corroborative information, Cichy now believed he knew the answer to the medical controversy surrounding the issue of Chopin's disease. He just needed to prove it.

For many years, Cichy had witnessed the profound depression and despair experienced by his cystic fibrosis patients. With few available role models and facing the grim expectation of a drastically shortened lifespan, those afflicted with this disease can often find it extremely difficult to fathom much that is noble or noteworthy about their existence. Cichy reasoned if he could prove that Frédéric Chopin, the most famous and recognized of all Poles, accomplished so much despite bearing the burdens of his genetically acquired disease, he would finally secure a near-perfect role model that had the potential to provide added hope, motivation, and inspiration for his many patients. Then, the main question: would he be allowed to proceed with his audacious quest? He would soon find out.

Minister Zdrojewski and Director Michalski, after a careful and considerate review, declined to sanction Cichy's study. Their rationale concluded, "This was neither the time to give approval, nor was it justified by the potential knowledge to be gained."[97] Also weighing heavily on the minds of those who made this decision was the relic-like status of Chopin's remains, as well as the question of the acceptance of such an analysis by the surviving relatives in the Chopin family tree. Michalski further stated, "The dominant view is the proposed research is going to serve first and foremost to satisfy the curiosity of the project's authors," while offering no "new knowledge that would have a meaningful impact on the assessment of the figure and work of Chopin."

What Michalski and Zdrojewski so astutely recognized was that currently available methods of DNA analysis are not foolproof in determining the clinical characteristics of cystic fibrosis. That is, even if a person's DNA were found to have some of the recognized mutations in his or her CFTR gene that would allow for the potential existence of at least some clinical manifestations of cystic fibrosis, those aberrant genes would not necessarily confirm any connection to the presence of a clinically identifiable disease. A person could possess the genetic mutations yet not have all of the symptoms of the disease. Diagnostic certainty would not be likely. This was the fatal blow to the investigator's request. As several of those involved with Cichy's team explained, "There is no easy way of finding out F. Chopin's final diagnosis. Even genetic analysis of DNA from Chopin's tissue could lead us into deceptive assumptions, unless two CFTR mutations were found."[98] Cichy himself told me that finding the mutations necessary for the presence of cystic fibrosis could be especially problematic if Chopin might have had a mutation in a gene other than those 1600 currently known. Uncertain about just what to look for and unsure about how they would interpret what they might find, Cichy and his team had faced an enormous challenge in their attempt to convince the authorities that access to the heart would provide a definite answer.

It's apparent the Polish team of investigators were inspired to search for the answer to the mystery of Chopin's illness not only by their curiosity about the identity of the famous composer's disease, but also by their wish to provide some consolation to the many present sufferers of cystic fibrosis, especially children afflicted with the disease. In fact, the more I think of it, the more I feel that this latter reason was their primary goal. As the investigators went on to state, "Is it justifiable to deepen our knowledge about the great Polish composer, but *foremost* [italics mine] to give hope and meaning to those who nowadays suffer from genetically inherited disorders? Is it not right to make an attempt to prove to many suffering people that many things count in life much more than a weak physical body, and that they are not predestined to vanish without leaving something that will influence, inspire and enrich the generations to come?"[99]

Is this a case of the ends justifying the means? If this rationale for an investigation were to become a precedent, then no end of bodies might be dug up in rather vain and over-justified efforts to assist the living cope with whatever limitation was genetically imposed upon them by their forebears. Cichy and his team indeed targeted a lofty and deserving goal, but the scientific shortcomings demonstrated in their proposed analysis of Chopin's DNA rendered their inquiry to be lacking the necessary prerequisites for a practical and accurate answer to the problem of identifying the composer's illness. Although Chopin and his preserved heart were at the center of the media attention, I don't believe the study was really designed to add any embellishment to his historic legacy. Furthermore, and more damning, in my opinion, Cichy's inquiry planned to focus exclusively on the DNA analysis for the presence or absence of cystic fibrosis. None of the other numerous diagnostic possibilities that have been considered for Chopin was to be investigated in his study. To me, this was a shockingly disturbing omission. The wise course of action was and still is to await the scientific knowledge necessary to provide a comprehensive and valid analysis. Despite my keen desire to know what it was that killed Chopin and my strong craving for closure in the search for his illness, deep in my heart I believe the Polish government acted wisely.

For the present, and while denied the necessary access to Chopin's remains to conduct the type of scientific analysis that might lead to a firm diagnostic conclusion, let's now examine more carefully each of the two leading diagnostic possibilities, the two very different of tuberculosis and cystic fibrosis. Perhaps our further understanding of these diseases might still enable an indirect conclusion, one accomplished without having to resort to the messy business of tissue procurement and its subsequent analysis. In other words, we won't wish to mess with Chopin's heart unless there is an excellent reason to believe probing the stiff fibers of this long-dead muscle will provide some reliably significant answers. In the event this proves impossible, our further knowledge would only help us better design an improved method of investigation, one more likely to gain approval from those who see as their sacred duty the eternal protection of Chopin's cherished identity and legacy.

Could Chopin Have Had "Consumption"?

*"The biggest disease today is not leprosy or tuberculosis,
but rather the feeling of being unwanted."*
Mother Teresa of Calcutta

During Chopin's lifetime, tuberculosis was one of the leading causes of death and disability. It was commonly referred to as *consumption* until a decade before the composer's death in 1849, when the new term *tuberculosis* was introduced and quickly became widely accepted. The old name had been popular for generations because it was an apt description of the terrible way the victims of this disorder appeared to be "consumed" from within. Despite its new appellation, however, there was scant new science to explain this ancient scourge. The many and confusing faces of this chronic pestilence had long delayed it from being recognized as a single entity. The exact cause of tuberculosis, its broad range of clinical characteristics, and its method of transmission would continue to baffle doctors for years to come.

It would be several more decades before scientists became convinced of the infectious nature of tuberculosis. It would take even longer to understand the multifarious manifestations of the disease. This difficulty in identifying the complexities of an illness and determining its causation is nothing new, the often painstakingly slow process having many similar precedents in the history of medicine.

Perhaps the most analogous recent example is that of the immunodeficiency syndrome now known as HIV or AIDS. As scientists struggled at the end of the last century to determine the cause of this sinister disease and observed with alarm the dramatic rise in its prevalence, they began alluding to it with a series of temporary designations. Some years later they settled on the term AIDS, but only after a great deal of research and methodological analysis. AIDS, like tuberculosis, is a wasting disease. And also like AIDS, tuberculosis can assume many different clinical forms, affecting its victims in quite diverse ways. Tuberculosis has long been referred to as the "great mimicker" for its ability to fool even the most seasoned physicians with its multiple pathologic presentations. It still manages to offer formidable challenges to the world's best physicians as they struggle to diagnose, treat, and then attempt to prevent the disease in the twenty-first century. In order to understand more about this complicated disorder and evaluate how closely its course might match the pattern seen in Chopin's illness, it's necessary to spend some time reviewing some basic information about it.

The disease now known to be caused by the bacillus *Mycobacterium tuberculosis* is truly a killer that has plagued humans from primordial times. Scientists studying the evolution of this sturdy microbe believe it was present in primate populations even prior to the presence of humans, and date its origins back as far as eight million years ago.[100] Thus, it's now recognized that tuberculosis has been present during all of human history, co-evolving alongside us and responsible for the deaths of untold millions of our ancestors. Its significance as a major cause of human death and disease throughout human history cannot be overstated. Even today, despite the advances of modern medicine and all the resources of the world's leading health organizations, tuberculosis has not gone away. The facts are sobering. It remains a deadly foe, every year infecting at least eight million and taking the lives of nearly two million.[101] Another startling statistic is that tuberculosis is the world's leading killer of women of reproductive age.[102] From the pharaohs of Egypt to Eleanor Roosevelt, from Alexander Graham Bell to George Orwell, this ancient adversary has cut a wide swath through human history, persistently remaining problematic to diagnose and treat, impossible to control and eradicate.

The current treatment of active tuberculosis is difficult, requiring for its success prolonged courses of multiple antibiotics, some with troublesome side effects and even the risk of death. Treatment regimens are rendered vastly more complicated by the fact that more and more cases of the disease are becoming resistant to the many antibiotics currently needed to combat it. The year 2008 saw the highest number of people infected with drug-resistant tuberculosis in history, some 1.5 million cases spread through 114 different countries.[103] These grim numbers continue to grow with each passing year. It also doesn't help matters that tuberculosis can often mimic other less serious and far more common illnesses, a feature leading to its being undiagnosed and untreated in millions more.

In many countries today, the most pressing problems in treating this major threat are due not only to the challenge of diagnosing the victims of tuberculosis, but also to the practical application of the prolonged treatment regimens required for its cure. Further contributing to this Herculean task is the absolute inadequacy of social resources sufficient to supervise these complicated and often somewhat risky regimens. Treating tuberculosis is not like taking a short course of pills and expecting to get well quickly. It requires a system of caregivers to monitor the usually lengthy treatment program, and this requires money and continual social support. This vigilant effort is necessary to ensure the compliance with treatment directives and to confirm their ultimate success or failure. Of course, with any delay in intervention, the disease only worsens in those afflicted and spreads to others. Today, tuberculosis remains an embarrassingly common disease, similar to its status in Chopin's day, and one not likely to go away any time soon.

The Church of the Madeleine in Paris where Chopin's funeral service was held.

Ten years after Chopin's death, the first tuberculosis sanitarium was established in what is now Poland. Similar to the spas he had visited in his youth, it could offer its afflicted visitors only "fresh air and prolonged rest." It's now difficult to imagine the enormous challenges a medical practitioner of Chopin's time would have faced when presented with a chronically ill consumptive patient. Being so woefully ignorant of the nature of tuberculosis and lacking the most basic diagnostic tools of investigation relied upon today, what could that practitioner do to provide *any* meaningful or helpful recommendations? One of the most helpful tools for the diagnosis and treatment of tuberculosis, the chest x-ray, would not be available for many years. It's no wonder physicians of Chopin's time did little else other than propose to bleed and blister their consumptive patients. They knew nearly nothing of this disease and were largely helpless in their efforts to combat it. Many of them would unknowingly contract the disease from their patients and share a similar fate.

When homeopathy was introduced into France in the 1830s, it did little to make any headway in fighting tuberculosis despite the many earnest hopes for a medical breakthrough, but at least its methods of treatment were benign. Fortunately for Chopin, the homeopathic practitioners he consulted toward the end of his life had largely discarded the old ways of harsh treatments, even if they had little else with which to replace them. The "first do no harm" motto must have regained its meaning for them.

We now recognize that tuberculosis spreads through the air when those who have the active disease cough, spit, or sneeze. However, not everyone exposed to the airborne particles becomes infected. Only about a fifth will succumb and develop the initial reaction, a respiratory infection not generally serious, and one that quickly becomes dormant in the vast majority of individuals.[104] This dormant infection, usually present in a tiny area of the lung, can remain latent in the body for many years, only to reawaken later and bring about active tuberculosis in, perhaps, only a tenth of those infected. Smoldering or latent infections can awaken and progress on to active disease under the influence of many factors, especially debilitating hunger, weight loss, and other forms of malnutrition. It's now recognized that dietary deficiencies can lead to a greater susceptibility to this active disease, with inadequate levels of vitamin D, B12, and iron leading the list.[105,106] Was Chopin's peculiarly restrictive childhood diet in some way responsible for his illness? Was he more susceptible than most?

The hemorrhagic coughing, known medically as hemoptysis, something Chopin is known to have experienced an untold number of times, is a frequent symptom of tuberculosis. It occurs in as many as 50 percent of infected individuals. The pattern of recurrent hemoptysis is a strong indicator of chronic bronchial inflammation and abnormality, and it indicates the bacterial infection has eroded its way into the branching blood vessels of the pulmonary tree. There are not too many diseases with such a pattern. Tuberculosis leads the list, followed somewhat distantly by cystic fibrosis, and then other causes of bronchiectasis, or bronchial abnormality. It has also been a long-observed phenomenon in tuberculosis that hemoptysis is consistently much more common in the winter months, especially the period between December and February, with its prevalence falling to very low levels during the warmer months.[105] This is precisely the pattern Chopin himself recognized. It was his main reason for his travel to the island of Majorca during that winter of 1838-1839. Additionally, these same studies have shown that hemoptysis often follows extreme changes in weather, especially changes in humidity. One of the worst episodes of hemoptysis Chopin ever experienced occurred during that same stay on Majorca and immediately followed an abrupt change in the weather and a major storm. Next time you hear Chopin's "Raindrop" prélude, the *D flat major* from *Op. 28*, think of the torrential rain pouring off the walls of the old monastery where he was holed up and its murderous effect on Chopin's bronchial tubes.

Another interesting piece of information derived from population studies of those with tuberculosis confirms that hemoptysis is more common in infected females, with the rate approaching 65 percent, but that increase is only observed during their first two decades of life, and then falls off quickly as they get older.[108] The males who are affected by this miserable calamity usually encounter it later in their lives. That these factors mimic the health events of the Chopin family could add further credence to the supposition that both Frédéric and his youngest sister, Emilia, suffered from tuberculosis.

Assuming Chopin may have been initially infected with tuberculosis when he was sixteen and then harbored the latent infection, were there factors that contributed to his developing the active form of the disease only several years later? Generally, the dormant interval is much longer, often decades. Was that a time of "malnutrition" in his life? Were other factors present that might have caused him to be so especially vulnerable?

Chronic alcoholism is a well-recognized risk factor for activating dormant tuberculosis. However, a close review of the historical record reveals that while Chopin enjoyed a glass of a good French Bordeaux, he was not alcoholic. Even considering the somewhat peculiar dietary recommendations of his family's physician, the malnourishment theory is difficult to accept. His parents were extremely concerned about his eating habits at that point in his life and probably would not have allowed such nutritional inadequacy. His family wasn't impoverished during those years and enjoyed a rather comfortable life without any evidence of extreme hardship. Did he have a concomitant disorder of digestion that rendered him malnourished despite a reasonable diet? If he did, that might point the diagnosis more toward cystic fibrosis, a disorder frequently accompanied by *malabsorption*, or an inability to absorb vital nutrients from one's food. If tuberculosis is still to be considered a leading candidate for Chopin's illness, some other factors must be invoked to explain the inconsistencies in its proposed hypothesis.

Genetic research has recently provided some interesting clues to the riddle of tubercular contagion that might help keep the tuberculosis theory alive. It has long been suspected that some individuals are more susceptible to acquiring the active form of the disease than others, for reasons not well explained by the malnutrition theories. It's now known that the susceptibility to acquiring tuberculosis can be heritable. Investigators have identified specific gene polymorphisms in the IL12B gene that are linked to an increased susceptibility to this disease.[109] The fact that Chopin's younger sister, as well as his father, died from what was believed at the time to be tuberculosis may indicate Chopin's family lineage carried this susceptibility. His older sister's death from an unidentified respiratory ailment at the age of forty-seven also could be supportive of this supposition.

The tuberculosis hypothesis for Chopin's illness could be sustained by this information. Through no fault of his own, Chopin perhaps carried within him a genetic defect, also present in other members of his family, which rendered him more susceptible to acquiring tuberculosis and more vulnerable to developing the more active form of the disease. There is no doubt the young Chopin had been exposed to tuberculosis. At times, he appeared to have been surrounded by people with the disease. His best friend of his youth, Jan Białobłocki, a boy with whom Chopin had spent much of his childhood, already suffered from the active form of tuberculosis as a teenager and died from it a few years later at the age of twenty-three.

Another close childhood friend, Janus Matusziński, also afflicted with this disease, would die in Chopin's own arms. Emilia's early acquisition of the disease and her rapid demise from an especially virulent form of the illness might also be explained by this unusual vulnerability.

Yet, if Chopin were especially endangered by tuberculosis and more defenseless to its advancement than most, how could he have possibly survived twenty-four more years with it? This prolonged course is especially unusual in view of the fact he received no known effective treatments, unless of course one believes in the therapeutic powers of bleedings, blisterings, acorn-water, and cream! Humor aside, discrepancies like this inject doubt into the widely held belief that tuberculosis was the cause of Chopin's sickness and death. Other options need to be explored.

Was it Cystic Fibrosis?

"A dry cough is the trumpeter of death."
Old French Proverb

W as cystic fibrosis, the hereditary disease affecting the mucus glands of the lungs, liver, pancreas, and intestines, the disease that Chopin suffered? That this disease is even considered to be a cause of his sickness and death still comes as a surprise to many Chopin scholars. Chopin's biographers, and there have been many, have largely accepted the tuberculosis hypothesis as gospel and have not elected to delve into the other possibilities. It is hoped that future writers, armed with more current information gleaned from scientific experts, will present a more balanced view in any discussion of Chopin's illness.

Following the Polish government's refusal in the summer of 2008 to allow access for the DNA testing of Chopin's remains for evidence of cystic fibrosis, there were front-page accounts of the story in news outlets around the world. It came as a bolt out of the blue to many readers of those articles that cystic fibrosis could even be contemplated in one who lived well into his adulthood. The controversy surrounding the investigation also quickly began to generate great interest among classical music lovers. While by no means certain to be confirmed as the disease that affected the Polish composer, cystic fibrosis does present an intriguing option, a postulate demonstrating many parallels to the pattern of his illness. To appreciate just how closely the new insights into this relatively unfamiliar disorder might apply to Chopin's story, it's necessary to spend some time reviewing this complex disease.

Although cystic fibrosis was not identified until the 1930s, it undoubtedly has been around for a long time. There exist a few historical descriptions of a similar illness dating from the Middle Ages.[110] The disease is caused by a mutation in the gene that regulates the transfer of sodium ions across cell membranes. To be specific, it's the CFTR gene, short for *cystic fibrosis transmembrane conductance regulator*. People with this genetic mutation have difficulty with the secretions in their lungs, pancreas, liver, and intestines, leading to various disease states. Mutations in this gene have been determined to go back many tens of thousands of years, with the speculation being that there most likely was once some survival advantage for those who harbored them.[111] It has been proposed that the same mutations that cause cystic fibrosis offered an added protection from cholera and tuberculosis, or even a greater ability to digest cow's milk long before humans evolved an easier way of doing so.[112] Those fortuitous advantages probably explain why mutations causing this uniformly fatal illness have managed to stick around for so long in human history. After all, doesn't evolutionary theory predict the survival of the fittest? Interestingly, the disease is limited only to Caucasians, with varying frequency in different populations. Furthermore, it's found more commonly among the people of Poland, occurring there in one out of every 2500 newborns. Cystic fibrosis is *the* most common autosomal recessive disorder of the world's Caucasian population, a surprising revelation to many.[113]

The clinical manifestations of cystic fibrosis are numerous and are a result of the pathological involvement of many different organ systems. Lung disease results from the clogging of air passages due to the buildup of sticky mucus, material that's always a magnet for bacterial growth and a contributing cause of pneumonia. Coughing up blood and heart failure are common in chronic cases. Thickened secretions in the pancreas and intestines only aggravate malabsorption, leading to poor growth and delayed development. This possible presence of nutritional deficiency was raised in the last chapter as a way to explain Chopin's theorized vulnerability to tubercular disease. Another unusual feature of this genetic disorder is infertility, affecting both males and females. While men with cystic fibrosis have normal hormone levels and all of the usual sexual characteristics, they lack the *vas deferens,* the tube connecting each testicle to the penis and hence cannot reproduce. Several of the scientific articles claiming Chopin had cystic fibrosis use this as one of their arguments to support their hypothesis and point to the fact that Chopin fathered no children.[114] Their absurd claims for his sexual promiscuity and resultant "proof" of his sterility have been previously refuted and will not be revisited here.

Other articles raise the issue of Chopin's difficulty growing whiskers on only one side of his face.[115] This peculiar tidbit of information is partly based on a humorous aside the twenty-one-year-old Chopin once wrote in correspondence to his family. He had joked that they needn't worry about the relative asymmetry of his moustache on the left side of his face, as that was not the side he displayed while performing in public. This statement has been seized upon as evidence of the composer's delayed puberty resultant from his affliction with cystic fibrosis. This assertion appears to be stretching things, considering the number of other fair-haired young men who anxiously worry about the adequacy of their beard growth at a similar age. As hormone levels in individuals with cystic fibrosis are normal, Chopin's relative lack of facial hair cannot be explained by an endocrine problem, unless one believes his sexual maturity was significantly postponed by the theorized presence of malabsorption and an associated developmental delay. While the hypothesis for Chopin suffering from malabsorption is a plausible one, there appears no firm evidence in the record to support that his sexual development was significantly delayed. Chopin's decision to underplay his sexuality was probably more a matter of choice than chemistry.

The hereditary pattern of cystic fibrosis and its possible effects on his family might do more to bolster the argument for its further consideration. Two of his three sisters died prematurely of respiratory disease. The symptoms in Chopin and his younger sister, Emilia, can be construed to indicate the presence of a disease with multi-organ involvement, an illness at times more characteristic of cystic fibrosis than tuberculosis. In addition, most people assume cystic fibrosis to be exclusively a disease of childhood, resulting in a life expectancy rarely extending past the age of twenty or, perhaps at the most, thirty. Although it's true that with the advantage of the best available care, survival can now be extended significantly longer, the fact remains that even with this advanced medical support, the median age at death for those with cystic fibrosis is still far too young. The idea of a childhood disease with a severely limited lifespan being the entity that affected Chopin appears unsupportable without some new information about this malady.

The cystic fibrosis hypothesis remains alive and still possible when one learns of the more recent discovery that adult forms of the disease can and do exist.[116] Since the discovery of the CF gene by Riordan in 1989, approximately 1600 mutations in this genetic assemblage of DNA have been uncovered, some resulting in unique clinical patterns of cystic fibrosis not previously recognized. These newly observed mutations occasionally allow for a disease with considerably attenuated clinical characteristics. That is, these forms of cystic fibrosis may not be nearly as severe as the disease ordinarily seen in children, and their symptoms may not become clinically evident until adulthood. It's now recognized that some adults presenting for the medical investigation of infertility, much to their subsequent shock and chagrin, fearfully learn they are suffering from cystic fibrosis.[117] Similarly, adults with multiple nasal polyps or otherwise unexplained lung disease are sometimes discovered after repeated medical visits and extensive testing to have this disease.[118]

When I was a young boy I remember a distant friend of mine having cystic fibrosis, and so, rather unknowingly, I witnessed the course of his life as I grew up. While most of us were running around playing hide-and-seek, baseball, or soccer, he was mostly confined to his oxygen tent, never once being able to participate in the usual play of childhood. Unfortunately, he never lived to see his fifteenth birthday. I suspect this is the tragic condition most of us think of when we hear mention of this dreaded disease.

When I was in my medical training and serving in a large pediatric hospital, I'd see these sick youngsters on the cystic fibrosis ward, or rather, I'd hear them hack and wheeze, desperately fighting their latest in a long line of terrible lung infections. Most of them were destined for a brief life, even with what then was the best medical care in the world. Today, many people – including many physicians – continue to have the same impression that I had then. This will need to change.

The current impossibility of testing for each of the multiple mutations of cystic fibrosis and the rapid advancement of analytic methods mean the likelihood of diagnosing more and more people with milder forms of disease in future years is quite high. The sheer number of these many mutations makes their detection in any detailed DNA analysis of Chopin a formidable challenge, one not currently possible with available technology. Obviously, cystic fibrosis can be a subtle disease, one often very difficult to diagnose in the living and even much more so in those long dead.

The case for Chopin being a sufferer of cystic fibrosis takes on added credibility with this new evidence for an adult-onset form of the disease. Many of the dilemmas of this investigation could be explained by this theory. He and his sister might have inherited a common disease, yet each with distinctly separate genetic mutations of their CFTR gene. That they each experienced such a different clinical course could therefore be explained. Chopin's survival to the age of thirty-nine could be explained by this hypothesis, as can the subsequent, somewhat premature, death of his oldest sister, Ludwika, who died at the age of forty-seven from an unexplained respiratory ailment.

The puzzling postmortem findings related by Dr. Cruveilhier do not now seem so enigmatic if cystic fibrosis replaces tuberculosis as the diagnosis. It's doubtful whether Cruveilhier would ever have witnessed the postmortem pathology present with cystic fibrosis and, if so, he certainly would have been sorely perplexed to understand it. The heart failure caused by cystic fibrosis could most assuredly have caused the enlarged heart he observed at Chopin's autopsy, but the typical findings of tuberculosis in the lungs, so readily recognizable to an expert like Cruveilhier, would have been strangely missing. What else could the famous anatomist have done but to sign off the case as just another example of that common consumptive scourge that surrounded him every day?

Consider the fact that Cruveilhier was then the premier expert on tuberculosis in all of France. His patient had been none other than the famed Frédéric Chopin, the frail composer and pianist commonly assumed to have long suffered from tuberculosis. Cruveilhier was compelled to write something on the death certificate. To write "cause of death unknown" was not acceptable protocol at the time, nor is it today. The physician was then and now still is required to give his or her best shot at the diagnosis and enter the most reasonable determination. Yet what happens when the disease in question hasn't been discovered or even described? What purpose would be served by postulating some postmortem mystery diagnosis amidst all the public outpouring of grief for the beloved composer? Chopin's family and his public certainly must have wished for closure. I think most can surmise how Cruveilhier might have responded to this pressure. He probably took the safe road in declaring tuberculosis as the cause of death, and consigned his insecurities over the matter to his private correspondence, using the halting phrases only he could decipher.

As there are problems posed by the theorized hypothesis that tuberculosis was the disease that killed Chopin, there are inconsistencies in the cystic fibrosis supposition as well. One of the most perplexing is the total lack of clubbing in the composer's fingers, a physical finding incontrovertibly preserved for posterity in the plaster casts of his hands that were taken by his son-in-law immediately after his death. Both tuberculosis and cystic fibrosis can cause this physical phenomenon, yet many clinicians claim its absence in someone dying from the respiratory insufficiency of cystic fibrosis is so unusual as to cast serious doubt on the accuracy of that diagnosis.[119] This missing physical component constitutes a major flaw in the proposal that cystic fibrosis was Chopin's disease, and it prompts a continued review of other possibilities.

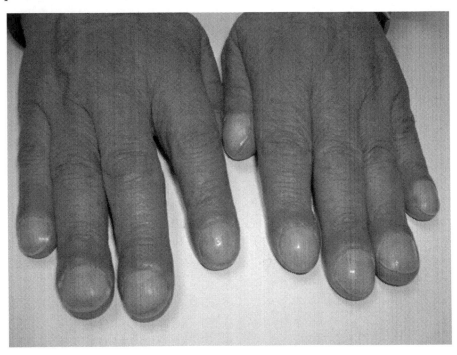

A photograph of a person's hands showing the clubbing phenomenon.

There has been little doubt among modern medical investigators reviewing the Chopin case that he suffered from a condition known as *congestive heart failure.* It's a common medical condition in today's world and probably was also seen fairly frequently in Chopin's time. Heart failure is more of a syndrome or a collection of physical problems than a disease by itself, and it needs to be defined by the diseases that cause it. Some common causes of heart failure may include a failed heart valve, a disease of the heart muscle itself, forms of advanced lung disease, and diseases of the *pericardium*, the thin membrane covering the outside of the muscular organ. Certainly, both cystic fibrosis and tuberculosis cause severe lung disease and thereby can lead to heart failure. Tuberculosis can also at times directly invade the heart muscle itself and lead to a condition called *cardiomyopathy*, another fairly common cause of heart failure.[120]

One of the newer theories about Chopin's illness maintains that he may have suffered from a disease of the pericardium. This theory submits that Chopin had a rather limited case of tuberculosis that involved only the upper lobes of his lungs and the pericardial sac.[121] His pericardium might have become so damaged and thickened by this disease over time that it acted like a glove stretched too tightly over the heart's surface. This squeezing of the heart then led to its subsequent failure. By being rather restricted to the heart and the difficult-to-examine upper regions of the lungs and larynx, the findings at autopsy might have been rather minimal for a person assumed to have suffered extensive pulmonary tuberculosis. Yet Cruveilhier should have been able to detect this if he were truly the expert he was reputed to be. The other theory asserts that Chopin's heart muscle was seriously weakened by the invasion of the tuberculosis bacterium into its own muscle fibers, a condition also leading to heart failure. This latter condition could have fooled any expert at autopsy, including Dr. Cruveilhier.

There could be more clues to the diagnosis of cystic fibrosis with a detailed DNA analysis of Chopin's remains. However, delving further into the investigation of the multiplicity of DNA variations gets technical, and it's beyond the scope of this book. There is also the issue of which DNA to study. Most scientific studies of ancient tissues now focus on mitochondrial DNA analysis, as it usually offers many more clues. Unlike the more familiar autosomal DNA, which people inherit as a jumbled recombination of genetic material from both parents, mitochondrial DNA is only passed down from mothers to children. The difficulties and limitations of current DNA testing will be addressed in a following chapter. Suffice it to say, absolute certainty for the diagnosis of cystic fibrosis and its multiple clinical presentations with DNA testing is not always possible and eludes even the most skillful and careful efforts of dedicated researchers.[122,123]

Without resorting to the detailed scientific analysis of Chopin's remains, further inquiries may not be able to provide satisfactory answers to these and other questions. The recent refusal by the Polish government to authorize the pathological investigation proposed by Wojciech Cichy and his Polish group of scientific investigators speaks more to the present-day inadequacies of DNA analysis than to any significant deficiencies of the team. It also has forced a closer reexamination of the Chopin historical record for any previously overlooked and subtle clues that would permit, however indirectly, a more complete understanding of what it was that took Chopin's life. Any present attempt at further analyzing the options must proceed without the disinterment of his remains, as that process currently constitutes an unpleasant prospect for some and one marked by ethical, cultural, religious, political, and social barriers, not to mention the numerous scientific obstacles. For the present time, Chopin's heart will continue to rest untouched in its stony niche.

At this stage in human history, science cannot promise to deliver definitive answers to this question, even if provided with the best available material evidence on a silver platter. Until that time arrives when a more precise analysis is available, we are left with speculation and hypotheses. However, it's in the best interests of this investigation that we begin the process of planning and designing a method for any future scientific analysis, one designed to seek as many answers as possible with the most minor disruption to Chopin's treasured heart.

Does it Matter?

*"I am convinced that it is not the fear of death, of
our lives ending, that haunts our sleep so much
as the fear...that as far as the world is concerned,
we might as well never have lived."*
Harold Kushner

Does it really matter what illness caused Chopins death? Does it matter that he slowly succumbed to a chronic rather than an acute illness? Would his music have been different had he enjoyed the benefit of good health? Would posterity have thought differently of him had he died quickly from a stroke, a heart attack, or perhaps as a result of some unfortunate accident? These are difficult questions, probably unanswerable. The peculiar hues on the palette of Chopin's existence, arrayed as they were with the separation from his family, exile from his homeland, rejection by the great loves of his youth, a devastating chronic illness, and the prospect of an early death, combine to color our final portrait of the man with dark and somber tones. Our lasting impression of him and his musical legacy must come from consideration of the many influences posed by this unusual amalgamation of emotional despair, chronic disease, and phenomenal talent. Attempting to separate these uniquely blended factors in an attempt to recognize which might have had the greatest effect at any given time in his life presents an enormous challenge.

In any historical analysis of Chopin's musical achievement, it's difficult to ascertain the degree of influence his long struggle with illness had on his compositional style. By now, you have discerned my repeated assertions propounding that his illness most definitely affected the character of his music, the number of works he was able to compose, and certainly the length of his career, both as a performer as well as a composer. That said, it's exceedingly hard to tease out the influence of his other experiences on his work. Unfortunately, his life was filled with enough disappointment, drama, and despair that the challenge of determining just which event may have done what, if anything, is daunting. There were, however, two major events of his young adult life that played critically important roles in shaping his character and emotional development. As if his self-imposed exile from his beloved Poland and his enormous sense of loss weren't bad enough, there was also the crushing rejection by the love of his life, the young Polish beauty, Maria Wodzińska.

Chopin's relationship with Maria extended back to their early childhood, and his reacquaintance with her in 1835 must have rekindled his warm memories of his own youth in Poland. The happy and intimate times he spent with Maria and her family encouraged him to spend long hours improvising and composing at the piano, and led to his writing the *Ballade in G minor, Op. 23,* a lovely piece filled with warmth, gaiety, and charm. It's one of his happiest pieces. With his proposal of marriage to Maria, he also seriously entertained a return to his beloved homeland, and with it the prospect for domestic bliss and an escape from the rigors of a career filled with concertizing. The return to the comfortable life of a composer, however attractive it may have seemed at the time, only revealed the young Chopin's naiveté, as its choice would have been fraught with financial insecurity, something Maria's parents undoubtedly anticipated with trepidation. Their protracted deliberation over whether to consent to their daughter's marriage meant Chopin was forced to spend uncertain and anxious months waiting for their eventual decision. When it finally came, the effect was devastating. His loss of Maria changed his life. Not only did their refusal to allow him to marry Maria increase his concerns about his frail health, but it probably also reinforced his resolve to be accepted into the highest circles of Parisian society, a social position the Wodzińskis never would have imagined possible for the struggling young musician they had so intimately observed in their home.

Yet his fate would include even more misfortune with an additional burden for him to bear. As a young man, he would also be forced to face a future made much more uncertain by the presence of the physical struggle with a chronic disease. He had already personally witnessed the tragically dramatic death of his younger sister, Emilia. He also had learned of the death of his good friend, Jan Białobłocki. He knew both of them had died of consumption, a disease he must have realized was seriously considered in connection with his own heath problems. He must have known he might be destined for the same end. The steady decline of his health following his self-imposed exile from Poland, and with it the abrupt loss of his close family support, and then the painful rebuff of his youthful love all combined in an indistinguishable manner to imbue both Chopin's personality as well as his music with an indefinable yet uniquely characteristic tone of melancholy. The Poles have a unique word for this heavy-hearted nostalgic state of emotion, the untranslatable, "żal."

Although Chopin's musical style changed remarkably little over his years, his later works displayed less of the showy brilliance of his youth and came to possess a more contemplative character. This melancholic tinge, although certainly apparent in his earliest works, would become increasingly common in those written later in his life. Ten years prior to his death, he would write to a friend to say "It would be good if I could still have a few years of big, completed work." Fortunately, he did and was able to crank out such gems as the lovely *Barcarolle,* the *Berceuse,* the Sonata for Cello and Piano, his major *Sonata, Op. 58,* the brilliant *Polonaise, Op. 53,* the meandering *Polonaise-Fantasie,* an interestingly introspective scherzo, the *Ballade No. 4,* and many others.

Daguerreotype of Chopin, probably taken in 1847.

His *Ballade in F minor, Op. 52*, one of his last great compositions and one of Western music's finest jewels, contains moments of rarefied beauty nuanced with seemingly multiple reflections on the past and a resigned acceptance of his death. There can be little doubt that at least a few of these late works gained more of this somber and reflective style following the composer's multiple and increasingly frequent encounters with the physical ordeals of a life-changing chronic illness. Many of his works are structured in such a way as to pit two diametrically opposing themes against each other. Often one theme is terrifying in the extreme, virtually screaming at times, while the other glides gently along like a lullaby, nearly a nocturne. Is it too much of a stretch of the imagination to believe that some of these might have recapitulated his long struggle with his own mortality? I think not.

In Chopin's era, it wasn't uncommon for someone to die at an early age. Many of Chopin's musical contemporaries were also afflicted with maladies that cut short their careers, if not their lives. Shortly after he arrived in Paris in 1831, Chopin had again been fascinated to witness the musical genius of Niccòlo Paganini. He had first heard this amazing and acrobatic Italian violin virtuoso perform in the summer of 1829 while still in Warsaw and had been absolutely mesmerized by Paganini's relaxed poise and technical mastery. The enormously impressed young Chopin quickly thereafter attempted to apply some of the same dazzling feats to the piano that Paganini revealed with his violin. Paganini at the time enjoyed great acclaim for thrilling audiences with his extraordinary performances that would demonstrate his wholly original and unorthodox style. Craftily sanding down his violin's strings before his concerts so that they would break under a predictable amount of pressure, he would daringly continue to play on, ultimately using fewer and fewer strings until he wound up performing pieces of amazing complexity on only one or two! He had quickly become a sensation due to his astounding degree of musical ability that he so skillfully combined with an abundance of showmanship. In addition to his string trickery, the lanky longhaired violinist would sport dark blue-tinted glasses to accentuate his rather ghoulish appearance on stage.

Tragically, Paganini was forced to withdraw from concertizing around 1834 for reasons of health. Rather suddenly, he had lost the fluid finger coordination so vital for his superb violin performances. A victim of syphilis, he had been receiving the common treatment of the time, compounds of mercury, potentially toxic agents that ultimately became responsible for his impaired coordination and confusion. Whether he was incapacitated by mercury poisoning or syphilis, or most likely both, Paganini was forced to end his career prematurely. Speculation also exists to this day that Paganini might have been afflicted with *Marfan's Syndrome*, a genetic abnormality responsible for many unusual physical abnormalities, among them greatly elongated fingers, a distinguishing feature Paganini was known to possess and use in a way ordinary people could not.[124] Paradoxically, the violinist's health issues may have worked both for and against him. There may be some interesting parallels here with Chopin's life story.

Niccòlo Paganini, the famous Italian violin virtuoso.

There are at least several instances in the history of music that serve to illustrate how a composer's battles with illness affected his musical works and compositional style. Beethoven's last works, full of intellectual depth and innovative expression, might never had been written in that unique style had he not been both seriously ill and profoundly deaf. The French composer Claude Debussy, who, like Chopin, suffered from a long and difficult battle with a fatal illness, demonstrated a notable change in his last compositions as his death grew nearer. A careful listening to his last works reveals telltale clues to his melancholy, disclosing music characterized by a much leaner style and filled with unique and rather strange dissonances. Debussy's second set of *Préludes*, written around 1913 in the *avante garde* style, is especially characteristic. In them, the composer pared down the music to its absolute essence without sacrificing any of its emotional depth. Following these intriguing works, the increasing doses of morphine necessary to control the composer's pain from widespread rectal cancer thwarted any of his repeated yet vain attempts at further composition.

Another French composer, Maurice Ravel, began to compose in a distinctly different style shortly after being involved in a serious car accident in which he suffered a head injury. Previously known for composing lively and dynamic pieces full of rhythmic diversity and brilliance, Ravel's style rather suddenly changed. What followed were works of an altered style, with rather strikingly different tonal and rhythmic characteristics. Only much later was it discovered that the well-respected composer was suffering from a type of selective dementia, unrelated to his previous accident, sufficient to explain the observed transformation. I find it remarkable that he was able to compose these still quite decent works considering his limitations.

These artists all suffered an inexorable decline in their health, and it was reflected in the style of their compositions. Although by no means should their health issues be considered to be the most influential among many imponderable others, they certainly played a significant role in the lives of these composers.

Far luckier and in great contrast, healthy individuals are probably content to live their lives largely free from great angst about what malady might end their days, preferring to be preoccupied with matters of their daily grind and personal affairs. When asked, many would rather focus their energies on the present rather than on trying to solve some unknowable morbid riddle about their future. Accepting the enigma of existence, many would most likely say something like, "Let that remain a mystery, and allow me get on with my life." Excluding suicide, the cause of any person's death usually does remain a mystery whose final clues often are only revealed during one's final moments, quickly and unpredictably. It's just another fact of our existence we must learn to accept; yet, living with the fear of death and being preoccupied with it must have its consequences.

To an admirable extent, Chopin tried to follow the path of peaceful acceptance, coexisting and tolerating the ignominy of his illness. His characteristically strong sense of wit and often self-deprecating humor no doubt helped him. He would frequently poke fun at himself and use a fair degree of denial in living with his infirmities. He was successful in compartmentalizing many of his concerns over his failing health and to a great extent was able to devote his dwindling energies to composition and teaching. His sometimes agonizing hours spent composing reflected his amazing ability to focus on a task and ignore distractions, apparently including concerns about his health. Chopin may not have been the most stoic of individuals, yet he did resign himself to his illness with a great amount of dignity and grace.

As a person's character is defined by everything predating death, where is the rationale of dwelling only on the cause of those final agonal moments? Shouldn't our eventual assessment of someone hinge more on one's personality, deeds, and accomplishments achieved during a lifetime than whatever proves to be his or her fatal pathology? It depends. This way of thinking, with its de-emphasis of the cause of death, applies mostly to individuals whose ends come rather quickly. Not everyone is so lucky. It doesn't always fit very well for those whose struggle with death is prolonged, as with Chopin. How different would the historical value of the cause of someone's demise be if that death came slowly, spanning not just days but decades?

I think most would agree that the degree of importance given to one's final illness must be linked to how acutely that terminal course plays out. In other words, an abrupt end without much premonitory warning, the way most of us would prefer to have our lives extinguished, can usually be given rather short shrift when it comes to amassing any lasting historic significance. An interesting exception to this argument must certainly be the apocryphal story of Louis Moreau Gottschalk, the famous nineteenth century American virtuoso pianist who, while performing on stage in Rio de Janeiro, suddenly collapsed on the keyboard and died immediately after finishing his dramatic piece, *Morte!*[125] Certainly, that was a manner of sudden death difficult to forget![126]

A chronic illness can transform a person's life, especially if it becomes the long-anticipated and likely cause of one's premature death. Such a fatal illness suffered over an extended period of time and one associated with lifestyle decisions, pain and suffering, great financial loss, or mental and physical disabilities often does have a profound effect on one's personality and character and consequently assumes a major role in any historical assessment. I believe Chopin's chronic suffering and expectation of an early death did play such a major role in his life, affecting many of his relationships, decisions, and, without doubt, his composition. His slow dance with death lasted decades. You can hear it in his music.

Much of the significance given to how life ends also depends on just how a person contemplates his or her death. Some may become so fixated on it that they cannot avoid a continual dread of their nonexistence, being nearly paralyzed by that fear. A good example of this is illustrated by the story of the great Russian composer, Sergei Rachmaninoff. For many years, he was afflicted with an obsessive fearful worry about death and would surprise his friends whenever he managed to *not* talk about it. This apprehension would influence many of his compositions. Apparently, he was not only terrified by his own mortality, but also that there might be survival after it!

Another famous Russian, Dmitri Shostakovich, no stranger to the theme of death, which he expressed frequently in many of his hauntingly beautiful works, believed the fear of death to be one of our deepest feelings, adding: "The irony lies in the fact that under the influence of that fear people create poetry, prose and music; that is, they try to strengthen their ties with the living and increase their influence on them."[127]

Once afflicted with a serious illness, especially one impossible to shake or mend, a person may react in myriad ways. Some might face this enemy with steely denial or even anger. I can see Beethoven shaking his fist at the heavens in his dying moment. I think of the Welsh poet Dylan Thomas instructing his father, "Do not go gentle into that good night" and then, "Rage, rage against the dying of the light."[128] Interestingly, Thomas also suffered from chronic health problems and died at the same age as Chopin. Rachmaninoff, like many so obsessed, couldn't rid himself of his morbid dread, and in his fear repeatedly kept reworking the ancient ecclesiastical chant for the dead, *Dies irae* ("God's wrath"), into much of his music. Still others might take a middle course, demonstrating realistic appraisals of their futures, and try their best to brace themselves for ordeals out of their direct control. More likely, some combination of all the possibilities occurs, the exact mix depending in large part on those protective psychological defense mechanisms related to the strengths and weaknesses of one's personality.

Faced with a certain death and a terribly uncertain life span, yet somehow surviving and thereby forced for many years to confront his illness, Chopin must have come to create his art as an act of defiance of death, attempting at times to distract himself from an obsessive worry over it and, in other moments, attempting to transcend it. Although he would eventually succumb to his illness after a long and difficult struggle, he would use his fear of death in some degree to advance his art, measure by measure.

Will Chopin's heart ever provide us the answers to our questions about his illness? Or will it be forever shielded from any intrusive analysis by our perpetual embarrassment in fooling around with a relic we still judge to be nearly sacred after all these years? It's only a piece of dead flesh and no longer connected to a body or in any way functional, yet we consider it to be almost holy, untouchable in the extreme. Is this an appropriate decision in this time of iPads, space shuttles, and Viagra? Let's look at this more closely.

Sacred Heart?

"The eternal mystery of the world is its comprehensibility."
Albert Einstein

The word "sacred" refers to someone or something worthy of religious veneration. In more everyday parlance, it can signify that whomever or whatever acquires this designation is "hands off" or "untouchable" for all practical purposes. Its designation erects an invisible and sometimes mysterious barrier to ordinary logic and convention, but does this unseen curtain also shield its beneficiary from the sometimes harsh light of scientific inquiry? In a strictly orthodox way of thinking, the answer is most certainly yes. Accordingly, in order to provide a justification for the disruption of a cherished object some consider sacred, it helps to do everything possible to demystify it. The currently sensitive issue of whether to proceed with the scientific analysis of the preserved heart of Frédéric Chopin needs for this relic to be divested of any imagined holiness and the study exposed for what it really is—an archeological investigation of a familial genetic disease.

There can be no doubt that Chopin's heart is a mighty symbol of the indomitable power of music to enlighten the human experience. For some, it can represent the courage and spirit of a nation besieged by loss. For others, it may render manifest their nonverbal feelings of nostalgia, love, national pride, and stubborn determination in the face of adversity. Still others may simply view it as a present-day reminder of the greatness of human achievement. However, for Professor Cichy and his team of scientific investigators, the investigation of Chopin's heart offers a marvelous opportunity to expand on that legacy by offering countless thousands of those currently afflicted with an incurable genetically acquired disease a stirring example of what accomplishments might be possible despite living with such a compromising malady. Essentially, what's the point of glorifying some profoundly honored symbol if it cannot be used for some transcendental purpose?

The concept of sacredness also broaches the complex issues of identity and privacy. Just as developing a fingerprint database once threatened entire societies with the loss of respect for civil rights and the right to privacy, the present rapid advance of DNA analysis, for some, preordains the implementation of genetic determinism, the fear that everything there is to know about an individual will be catalogued and scrutinized by an ominous regulatory authority.

The extraordinarily popular use of ABO blood typing in Japan as a purported way of revealing personality and character traits is a good example of how genetic analysis is being misused in an unanticipated way. In current day Japan, a person's blood type is considered a significant determiner of a person's character traits. Employers often will use this hematologic pattern to screen out those who they believe are "undesirables." Matchmaking agencies exploit this personal information to connect lonely singles with mutually desired traits. Despite the fact that this wholesale application of genetic typing for the delineation of a person's identity has been repeatedly and roundly debunked by legions of scientists, its acceptance by the general public is widespread and growing. There is a weird sense of mysticism attached to this rather simple example of genetic analysis, and it also extends to the new field of DNA typing technology. Is this simply voodoo science, or is there some justification for it?

Sadly, the general understanding of genetics by much of society lags far behind the rapidly expanding body of scientific knowledge, making naïve presumptions all too common. The opaque screen of incomprehension, so essential for the acceptance of the sacred, also shrouds this increasingly important modern science.

DNA typing technology is now advancing at a pace reminiscent of the exponential growth in computer microprocessing. DNA identification is now regularly used to identify victims of crime or catastrophe, establish paternity and family relationships, match organ donors, identify criminals, and exonerate people wrongly accused. It is used to identify bacteria that may pollute air, water, soil, and food. It can even be used to authenticate consumables such as wine and caviar!

DNA analysis has become an essential element in archeology's modern arsenal in reconstructing the lives of ancient peoples and in understanding the intricacies of human evolution. What first began in the public arena of forensic reviews of criminal cases is now being applied to private archeological studies of ancient civilizations. The term forensic begs to be better explained. It's simply a methodology for seeking information in family, civil, and criminal matters when used within a legal context. Good examples of forensic archeology are the use of DNA analysis to identify the victims of mass burials in Iraq or the "Disappeared Children" of Argentina, all victims of atrocious crimes once irrecoverable by standard investigation.

A better term for the science of using these methods for archeological use is the recently introduced *bioanthropology*. This new scientific endeavor represents the combination of traditional anthropological methodology and modern molecular genetics, joined together with corroborative evidence from other fields such as archeology, epidemiology, histology, and history. Whether used to chart the course of the great ancient human migrations across the globe, to search for the suspected presence of a cleft palate in King Tut, or to reveal the details of North American turkey domestication, DNA analysis is an established science, accepted and here to stay.

Scientists were recently able to crack one of the great mysteries of European history by using DNA testing to prove that the son of the executed French King Louis XVI and Marie Antoinette had not escaped, as some had theorized, but actually had perished in prison as a child. In December of 1999, the presumed heart of this child was removed from its resting place for DNA analysis. Interestingly, there wasn't any public outcry over the removal of *this* child's heart and its subsequent analysis! Samples taken from both living and dead relatives of the royal family, including a lock of hair from his mother, Marie Antoinette, proved that this child was in fact the heir to the throne. The heart's DNA analysis must have offered great relief to those nervous French officials who secretly feared some future return of the royal monarchy!

In 1995, Robert Massie published an account of his investigation into the intriguing mystery of the Russian Imperial family, the Romanovs. For many years, a woman by the name of Anna Anderson had claimed that she was the surviving princess of the royal family, Anastasia Romonov, the youngest daughter of Tsar Nicholas II. She seemed to know so many of the private details of that family that no one could state categorically whether she was a fraud or the true article. Although Massie's work revealed no genetic match between Ms. Anderson and the royals, she steadfastly stood by her somewhat plausible story.[129] It would require another DNA analysis, this time conducted in 2009 by Dr. Michael Coble of the US Armed Forces DNA Identification Laboratory, to unravel this consanguineal mystery. Coble studied the scraps of human material gathered in 2007 near Ekaterinburg and proved conclusively that they were indeed the remains of the lost princess, murdered in 1918 by the secret Bolshevik police.[130] Finally admitting she had met her match with this exact science, Anna Anderson reluctantly relinquished her boastful claims to the blue blood of royalty.

Both of these studies proved the usefulness of mitochondrial DNA analysis. Testing of tissues containing cellular elements, usually well-preserved specimens of recent origin, is routinely done with several methods, yet these don't work for ancient specimens, where cellular components have nearly always deteriorated to a point far past their usefulness for these techniques. Mitochondrial analysis as applied to bone, teeth, and hair samples, however, is customarily utilized in these studies and undoubtedly will be instrumental in any study of Chopin's heart. Just which methods might be used will depend on the degree of preservation of that tissue. Silently soaking in its unknown brown brew, Chopin's heart still waits to tell its complete story!

Applying mitochondrial analysis to the study of genetic diseases in ancient specimens, like that proposed in the approach to Chopin's heart, has already been able to uncover some interesting information. Examining ancient skeletons in the Middle East, investigators have used this method of DNA analysis to determine the presence of an isolated mutation that once allowed for the spread of a common form of anemia in that population.[131] Finding the mutant gene, using the same process as that outlined by Professor Cichy in his proposal for Chopin's tissue, clinched the existence of this disorder. The rapid sophistication of these methods incorporating the newest scientific advances makes the application of these analyses appropriate for ever-broadening avenues of research. Even during the short interval of time from when Cichy first announced his plans in 2008 for testing on Chopin's heart to the present, there have been significant advances that could allow for an even less disruptive study. The steady advance of science is indeed relentless.

The differences in the genetic material between individuals are mind-bogglingly minimal. Humans share 99.9 percent of the same genetic matter; only about three million chemical molecules mark the genetic difference between any two people. Although one tenth of one percent doesn't sound like much, the varied patterns of those base pairs make for dramatically diversified humans. Just look around!

Most of that genetic matrix is of an unknown function. The vast preponderance of the human genome consists of sequences that most now believe have no medical or social value. Only a few genetic locations (loci) have been connected to recognized disease states, anatomical characteristics, or functional capabilities. However, this field is changing so quickly that major discoveries are occurring with increasing frequency. What appears to be worthless stuff today could prove to be indispensable material in the future! Forensic testing as currently applied has been strictly limited to those sequences that have no known implications for health, physical, and mental traits, but that can and undoubtedly will change. The issue of privacy and civil rights protecting one's genetic makeup, that sacred inner register of one's abilities as well as vulnerabilities, will become an immensely important issue in the years to come. That is, if one doesn't think it already is.

It's obvious that as science is increasingly able to probe the mysteries of the past and as more and more people accept a progressively more secular view of the world, the boundary between what's considered sacred and what's not is blurring. For some, that division doesn't even exist.

At this point an example from the past might be enlightening. The sixteenth president of the United States, Abraham Lincoln, still occupies a position of near-sacred reverence for many, not only in his own country but also across the world. Examining his legacy and the captivating details of what eventually happened with his embalmed body provide some interesting similarities with the case of Chopin. Both lived at about the same time in history. Both are regarded as legendary figures not only in their own respective countries but also around the world, and both were consumed by their preoccupation with their own country's internal struggles. They each created cherished works of art—Chopin with his finely polished music, and Lincoln with his beautifully crafted speeches. Chopin's preserved heart was trans-ported widely. Lincoln's embalmed body was moved seventeen times. Chopin's heart was the subject of intrigue and exploited by the Nazis. Lincoln's corpse was nearly stolen on Election Day, November 7, 1876, by an Illinois counterfeiting ring, intent on using the body for ransom. Will there be even more similarities?

In 1900, Lincoln's monument needed major repairs (the beautiful Lincoln Memorial would not be built until 1922). Stung by the painful memory of the near-disastrous theft of his father's body a quarter of a century earlier, Robert Lincoln carefully supervised the construction of the new monument and the removal and relocation of his father's casket, a simple pine box. There were some who doubted the actual presence of the former president's body and wished to exhume the con-tents of the coffin for confirmation of its identity. Others were squea-mish and felt that any such intrusion would only be disrespectful. They claimed that Lincoln's body was a near-sacred relic. Eventually, the decision was made to open the casket before its reburial. For the few who peered down into the small hole cut into the top of that decaying pine box on that day in September 1901, it was a terribly exciting yet rather gruesome task.[132]

After everyone present appeared satisfied that the body was indeed that of Abraham Lincoln, the casket was resealed, placed in a heavy steel cage, lowered ten feet underground, and then cast in a three-foot-thick enclosure of concrete. Robert Lincoln, upset over this latest and most intrusive episode in a long series of jarring disturbances to his father's tomb, took great pains to ensure that no one would ever again violate his father's final resting place.

The story of Lincoln's exhumation is instructive. Here is an exam-ple of the near-insatiable curiosity people have to reinspect and probe the past, regardless of the assumed sacredness of the object of their attention. It reveals the sometimes skewed degree of respect the public may hold for a family's privacy, and then exposes that family's resul-tant moral outrage elicited by such a conspicuous exhibition of their long-buried relative's remains. Does this sound familiar?

There are many other examples of archeological discovery involv-ing long-dead notable figures of history. Isaac Newton's remains were once analyzed and found to contain high levels of mercury, presum-ably from his work as an alchemist. Ludwig Beethoven's exhumation and subsequent forensic analysis provided ample material for Russell

Martin to claim that lead, used extensively by Beethoven's physicians in their attempts to correct the composer's many health problems, contributed to his physical decline and death.[133] These studies were undertaken long before DNA analysis become so sophisticated. Think of what else might have been learned about these famous individuals if this new scientific method of discovery had been applied to their tissues!

I think the case can be easily made that Chopin's heart is not sacred. His heart needn't be considered untouchable. There are now many established precedents for the examination of the remains of highly admired historical figures, examinations that have had absolutely no adverse effect on the continued veneration of their subjects. If anything, this additional information, gleaned from respectful and diligent analysis, has only added to their subjects' mystique. The widespread respect for Chopin's legend and his immortal legacy needn't necessarily preclude any authorized scientific study that attempts to learn more about the man himself through a careful analysis of his body's remains. The question in the end probably depends much less upon how sacred his heart is considered than it does about how much meaningful information a scientific investigation of its fibers might disclose about him. Our present scientific capability is getting very close to being able to boast, without equivocation, that the results of the DNA analysis on Chopin's heart will justify the means. Will they?

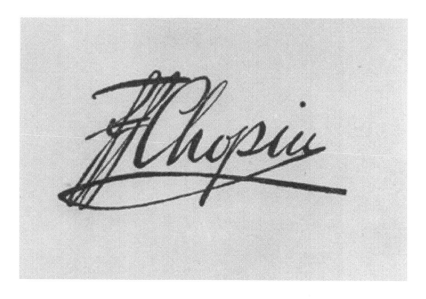

Chopin's elegant signature.

Let's take one last look at what it would mean to probe the secrets of Chopin's not-so-sacred heart. Perhaps now we can summarize all the possible associated problems and repercussions involved in such an analysis and then finally make a proposal as to how to proceed.

A Heartfelt Proposal

*"The future belongs to those who give the
next generation reason for hope."*
Pierre Teilhard De Chardin

It is now apparent to me that any final conclusion regarding the identity of Chopin's illness awaits a future scientific analysis of his remains. Deductive reasoning can take us only so far. As of 2010, approximately ten hypotheses have been raised to account for his disease. In my mind, the arguments for two or three lead the rest by a significant margin. Cystic fibrosis, tuberculosis, and alpha 1-antitrypsin deficiency now appear to be the most likely prospects, with each entity having its own rationale and advocates. Speculation is always possible, yet never brings with it a satisfactory consummation to our desire for certainty. If, and it's a big if, a consensus supporting a scientific methodological inquiry can be obtained, and a definitive answer is desired by the world's leading Chopin authorities, then the difficult work of obtaining sanctions and permissions for this investigative analysis can begin again.

The thorny questions as to whether to proceed with such an inquiry were prompted in 2008 by the request from Dr. Cichy and his team of investigators in Poland. His study planned for the removal of Chopin's heart from its interment in the Holy Cross Church of Warsaw, and the taking of tissue samples for DNA analysis. There was also planned to be an examination of the remains of Chopin's younger sister, Emilia, to be exhumed from her grave located elsewhere in the same city. Permission was also requested for DNA sampling from the two remaining living relatives of Chopin. The study's stated purpose was to determine, to the extent possible, the DNA composition of the Chopin siblings. Specifically, the investigators were looking for just two mutations of the CFTR gene. Would this analysis demonstrate compatibility with the diagnosis of cystic fibrosis?

These mutations in the CFTR gene were explicitly sought, as finding them would make the diagnosis of cystic fibrosis in these two individuals highly likely. Even with this intrusive and detailed analysis, however, certainty in achieving a firm clinical diagnosis for the composer was not by any means guaranteed. In fact, depending upon which CFTR mutations were found, the accuracy of achieving a solid conclusion for a plainly evident disease in the composer was recognized to be glaringly poor, even by non-scientists. Unraveling the various pieces of the genetic code, no matter how much one is awestruck over the reality of its actual accomplishment, is currently not yet sufficient to predict with any great accuracy the physical impact of cystic fibrosis. The very large number of possible genetic mutations that can produce variants of this disease currently make it impossible to state with certainty what that pathological picture may look like in any given individual. It appears the clinical expression of a particular genetic pattern can wear many different and, most frustratingly for scientists, quite unpredictable costumes! Unfortunately, this uncertainty is the current state of the art in attempting to use only DNA evidence for diagnosing the clinical manifestations of cystic fibrosis. Furthermore, any such analysis would be vitally dependent on the preserved state of whatever degraded tissue could be obtained, a condition far from certain in both of these specimens.

Chopin's heart had been immersed in an alcohol solution, according to the accounts following his death. Exactly what that concoction was is anyone's best guess. Some have claimed it was French cognac, much to the mirth of some and to the absolute disgust of others. In the 1840's, there weren't many alternatives. Formaldehyde, that efficacious but terribly smelly embalming fluid, wouldn't be invented for thirty more years. Just what type of alcohol Cruveilhier might have used is unknown, yet the choice is critical for adequate long-term preservation of bodily organs. The concentration of alcohol in any tissue preservative solution is fundamental to its success. If it's too low, the tissue deteriorates; too high, and the protein in the tissue becomes denatured, essentially scrambled and worthless for accurate microscopic analysis. Can a fine cognac really measure up to the challenge of this grisly task?

The last anyone had observed Chopin's heart was after World War II, when, after a complicated series of possessions, it was eventually examined by the Polish musicologist Bronisław Sydow. Untrained in medicine and ignorant of any of the necessary prerequisites for an adequate scientific analysis, he wrote a frustratingly brief report on the urn's contents: the heart appeared "perfectly-preserved."[134] He went on to state that the heart was "enlarged" and bathed in an "amber" liquid. Was that color due to the cognac itself or simply the telltale traces of the residual hemoglobin pigment in Chopin's blood?

Professor Cichy has also had the opportunity to read Sydow's full report, as provided to him by Sydow's present-day relatives (Bronisław Sydow died in 1952). For its own personal reasons, the Sydow family has firmly requested that Cichy and others not make any public disclosures about the contents of that report. However, Cichy has shared with me his opinion that Sydow's description of the heart does nothing to dissuade him from considering cystic fibrosis for Chopin's diagnosis. Accordingly, one can speculate that the report does not necessarily confirm a diagnosis of either tuberculosis or any other disease, or else Cichy and his team would not have launched their attempt to confirm the presence of the cystic fibrosis mutations. In other words, simply eyeballing the heart is not going to be sufficient to make the diagnosis!

The question remained: would Chopin's preserved tissue be of sufficient quality to allow for a detailed DNA analysis? This was an uncertainty Cichy's investigators were prepared to face. They probably believed some information would be better than none. And they obviously didn't view Chopin's heart to be the untouchable relic it was touted to be by some musical historians. In fact, they were prepared to approach the pope if the local Catholic parish or the Archbishop of Warsaw had decided to be an obstacle to their inquiry. I suppose their question to the pontiff would have asked if he felt the earthly remains of a non-saintly and non-practicing Catholic who died 160 years ago were for any recognizable reason in the Church's opinion still to be considered off-limits to a scientific analysis. The investigators must have thought they'd have a strong case. Cichy's team had truthfully believed the strongest objections to their investigative plans would come from the Church and were more than a little surprised when the final decision boiled down to a low-key and reasonable analysis done by couple of secular individuals. As it turned out, these were patient and intelligent people who, carefully and methodologically, had to compare the veracity of the team's expansive claims for a successful outcome with their own measured assessment of the likelihood of an uncontested conclusion from this controversial venture. They obviously felt that such a study would not be worth all the fuss and bother, all the disruption, all the public attention, if in the best of circumstances, the only answers that could be obtained by such an unsettling inquiry would merely be a long string of maybes and vague possibilities.

The remains of Emilia also presented obstacles to a careful inquiry. The adequacy of her decomposed tissues to shed light on the cystic fibrosis theory can be questioned. Suitable mitochondrial DNA can be obtained from many of the body's tissues, with bones and teeth being the best for analysis in older specimens. Obviously, these may be the only items available after so many years of disintegration and decay. DNA analysis of the hair is also possible, yet much depends on the adequacy of the sample, with the hair follicle or root being the most critical part. The hair follicle, that part of the hair where growth takes place, can be a potential gold mine for DNA analysis, with the hair shaft itself being a much inferior source. French investigators have recently been able to perform limited DNA sampling on ancient remains of mummies from the eighteenth and nineteenth centuries using only hair samples, but they had been lucky to find remnants of the intact hair follicles.[135] Yet even with this degree of luck in finding the intact follicles, the quality of that tissue would not have allowed for the more rigorous analysis required to find the CFTR mutations needed to diagnose Chopin's case. I have discussed this issue with Professor Michal Witt, the head of the Division of Molecular and Clinical Genetics at the Institute of Human Genetics and Polish Academy of Science in Poznan. We both agree that these ancient dusty specimens, devoid of their all-important follicles, would most likely not allow for an adequate DNA analysis.

Currently, there are at least two locations that have preserved specimens of Chopin's hair, the Fryderyk Chopin Museum in Warsaw and the Bibliothèque Polonaise in Paris. Other specimens are claimed to exist in Germany, Majorca and the United States. These specimens, ranging from chestnut brown to a pale dusty-blond, appear to be samples snipped from Chopin's locks after his demise and thus devoid of any intact follicles. However, it can be hoped that with future improvements in DNA analytical methods, these faded filaments might someday provide a more easily obtainable source of information. This might be especially important if the world remains squeamish about exposing his heart. There have been a couple of recent scientific reports using washed samples of ancient hair for forensic DNA testing, a new method of analysis that could possibly transform these musty old museum specimens into a tantalizing and readily available source of information for any future investigation. Any enthusiasm for analyzing these hair samples, however, must be tempered by the obvious realization that they cannot be conclusively proven to have come from Chopin!

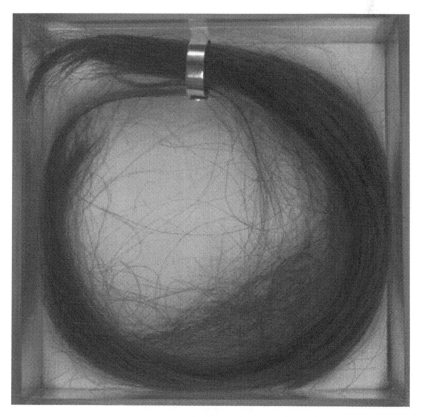

A sample of Chopin's hair.

From all accounts, the Polish team's sudden request for a methodological DNA inquiry into the identification of Chopin's disease forced the Polish authorities to conduct a careful and considered review of the investigation's possible merits and, to the absolute credit of all concerned, not its immediate and automatic rejection. Professor Cichy and his team of researchers from the Department of Forensic Medicine at Wroclaw Medical University had presented their proposal only to the Polish Minister of Culture and the Fryderyk Chopin Institute. Interestingly, the Catholic Church was summarily excluded from these deliberations. The Polish government apparently never felt it necessary to approach Warsaw's Archbishop Nycz or the Friars of St. Vincent de Paul of the Holy Cross Church as, at some point it had already decided not to allow the investigation to proceed further. This all fits with the investigators' belief that the Church would likely refuse access to these remains, and hence their decision to bypass the Church until after they first sought what they felt would be easily obtained permission from the Polish governmental authorities. Father Marek Białkowski, the local parish priest in Warsaw, claims he and other church authorities were never contacted.

According to Michalski, one of the two surviving Chopin relatives gave her consent for the DNA analysis of the heart but the other did not.[136] Within a year following the announcement of the scientific inquiry the assenting relative died, and with her death the fate of Cichy's polemical proposal was perhaps sealed. Irrespective of these family squabbles, however, Cichy's request for access to the heart was denied. The reasons given for its rather abrupt dismissal now seem scientifically reasonable even if one doesn't completely agree with the government's rather conservative conclusion. Ultimately, the Minister of Culture and the Director of the Institute of Fryderyk Chopin had to consider all of the ramifications of such a controversial study and the inevitable repercussions that undoubtedly would have attracted mixed reviews from all over the world.

The fact that plans were already underway for the many celebrations in 2010 of the two hundredth anniversary of Chopin's birth must have been a major factor influencing their decision. Any botched or inconclusive effort at this intrusion into the revered remains of the famous composer would have only provided a major embarrassment to all involved. Imagine those musical pilgrims at the Church of the Holy Cross, arriving in steady droves and breathlessly waiting to see where Chopin's heart lay buried, only to be shocked to see a small sign indicating that the precious organ had been removed for experimental research. The possibility of unfavorable public opinion only added to the Polish government's misgivings about the merit of the investigation and reinforced its eventual refusal to sanction it.

Any future requests and their subsequent reviews will be measured alongside this one. I fully suspect the sanctioning authorities have learned from this experience to be no less careful in the future. Any investigation of Chopin's heart or tomb is bound to open a virtual Pandora's box of problems, and may prove to be too difficult to launch. Any one of the many principals involved might move to blackball any inquiry. If family consent is refused, no amount of scientific rationale will matter. The sole surviving member of the Chopin clan now claims to be adamantly opposed to any investigation of her famous ancestor's remains, although she is quite elderly and may not be around to decide the fate of any future proposal. If the Church decides in its pious wisdom to refuse access to the crypt, it's likely no amount of governmental pressure or investigatory pleading will succeed in overturning that decision either.

To satisfy the many interested scientists whose curiosity has now been piqued by this enigma, the inquiry team, and it really *must* be a team of individuals with delegated tasks, needs to pass muster with the international scientific community of cystic fibrosis experts as well as DNA experts trained in the latest techniques. This constitutes a rather daunting challenge. In addition, any scientific party must possess the ability to search for *all* the listed diagnostic possibilities not just for the clues supporting its own pet theory. That is, the investigation must be sufficiently broad in its scope of scientific inquiry to include analytical techniques to search for clues to as many of the theorized diseases for Chopin's illness as feasible. Such a study looking for a range of possible diagnoses was not planned in Professor Cichy's proposal but needs to be actively considered for the next. Only then will it have the necessary breadth of scientific investigation to garner sufficient support for its acceptance.

In all likelihood, the team will need to have strong cultural ties to Poland and France. I believe that pretty well restricts the majority of the team's composition to either Polish or French scientists. Ideally, it would consist of parties from both countries, the investigation being part of their shared cultural heritage and interest. Professor Cichy informs me he will mount another attempt at an investigation of the heart immediately following the 2010 celebratory year. Currently, he does not have plans to conduct a full-scale investigation of the other diagnostic possibilities since his area of expertise is in cystic fibrosis research. He does say he is open to the idea of having a multidisciplinary committee determine what other diseases should be considered for Chopin's diagnosis. However, just who would have the authority to assemble this committee and direct its recommendations is far from clear at this point.

Even if a study can be sanctioned and a team assembled, any results it obtains might not be cut and dry. With any of the leading candidates for the disease responsible for Chopin's end, there needs to be some scientific accommodation. Not every piece of information from such an inquiry might precisely fit with all of the possible diagnoses and, like with so many of the fascinating medical mysteries I have encountered during years of medical practice, there always remain peculiar inconsistencies and idiosyncratic details.

I first appreciated this phenomenon during my freshman year in medical school while laboring late at night doing my dissections in the human cadaver laboratory. I would often stumble upon variations in human anatomy not described in the textbooks. My anatomy professors would simply smile knowingly and shake their heads and then patiently proceed to explain to their neophyte pupil the astonishing diversity and complexity of the human body. Later, in practice, I would sometimes observe patients who suffered from certain illnesses whose course would defy the typical predictions for their disease. There appeared to be a wide variability in the manifestations of these illnesses, often linked to the unique traits of those afflicted with them, making attempts at exact diagnoses and prognoses frequently a formidable challenge. Much to my amazement and delight, I continued to discover this unpredictability throughout my career. So when it comes to selecting a leading disease candidate for Chopin's illness, I can understand why the variability and complexity of his case has generated not one but multiple hypotheses. Frustratingly, a precise diagnosis for Chopin may always remain elusive.

I continue to vacillate between tuberculosis and cystic fibrosis to account for the disease that so altered the life of Frédéric Chopin. These two illnesses are similar in some ways, very different in others. They are both considered chronic diseases, yet they also can be responsible for the rapid death of those afflicted. Cystic fibrosis is exclusively heritable; tuberculosis, at least according to current information, is only sometimes so. Both cause chronic lung insufficiency, and both can lead to heart failure. Both are wasting diseases that can result in decades-long clinical courses. Both are marked by periods of relative stability at times punctuated by episodes of serious infections, bronchial hemorrhaging, and the risk of death. Both can cause multi-organ damage and a wide array of symptoms. Yet the pathological evidence left behind by each illness after a person's death is strikingly different. That is why Dr. Cruveilhier's off-the-record comments have been so jarring to the tuberculosis theory. The inconsistencies in his reports are glaring and cry out for a resolution.

The scientific beauty of the case and the often persuasive arguments for the diagnosis of cystic fibrosis are very appealing to me, and I must admit they possess some merit. However, the absolutely firm absence of any finger clubbing observed in the composer's hands is most troubling and forces me to rank this disease below tuberculosis in its likelihood of being Chopin's disease. To have cystic fibrosis from birth, even accepting that its full manifestations do not appear until late adolescence, and then to suffer it for twenty years and not demonstrate any clubbing seems to me most unlikely. The exact reasons for the appearance of clubbing are currently poorly understood and may turn out to be determined by genetic factors. If this is someday proven to be the case, then an argument could be made for how Chopin escaped this peculiar abnormality. Yet, despite this possibility, tuberculosis must remain my leading diagnosis for his disease.

Leaving aside the knotty issue of whether Dr. Cruveilhier and Ludwika conspired to suppress more accurate information about Chopin's disease, the autopsy findings, if we can really call the hurried removal of Chopin's heart an autopsy, are of concern. Even if we grant to Dr. Cruveilhier the extensive degree of knowledge of pathological anatomy he was purported to possess, a rushed and thereby cursory examination of the chest cavity might not have been sufficient for him to establish a firm conclusion. He may have been overly influenced by his narrow assumption that tuberculosis surely had to be the illness he viewed in the dying composer. That stubborn belief may have led to his failure to remain steadfastly objective during that hastily performed postmortem procedure. It was a cursory affair and he knew it. He didn't even take the time to write a report. Instead, he directed an attendant to jot down fragments of his meandering comments made during the procedure. In the end, Cruveilhier may have been merely voicing his guilt-ridden uncertainties about his disputable analysis to

Chopin's loved ones, never knowing the trouble it would cause generations of future investigators. As many modern doubts about the cause of Chopin's illness originated with Cruveilhier's shaky observations, they also could be put to rest by assigning a more critical eye to the supposed accuracy of the French anatomist's conclusions. With these suspicions in mind and considering all the currently available evidence, I now believe tuberculosis, albeit in an unusual manifestation, was the disease of Chopin. His many fine biographers, largely ignorant of any controversy, have been correct all along!

My investigation into the identity of Chopin's illness has only served to heighten my appreciation for both the man and his music. No matter which illness turns out to be the proven cause of his suffering, if in fact there ever is a study sanctioned to determine it, the fascinatingly complex qualities of his music continue to enthrall and enliven me. I find it truly breathtaking that he was able to continue to compose his masterpieces despite his prolonged and repeated episodes of serious illness. It's even more amazing to learn that he could accomplish all this despite his longstanding addiction to opium-containing cough remedies and their mind-addling effects! That he retained his wry sense of humor, his lively spirits, and was able to pen music of joyful abandon, as evidenced in his playful mazurkas, while facing such an uncertain future is duly impressive and inspirational. Chopin personified what it then meant to be Polish—misery concealed, suffering suppressed, strength arising out of adversity, character from endurance.

He must indeed have had a remarkable emotional ability to compartmentalize his anxieties, his grief, and his everyday troubles in order for him to have directed his intense focus on his enduring passion for composition. He has at times been portrayed as a rather weak man, indecisive, and a dandified snob of the Parisian salons. That he was a sometimes arrogant and haughty person, I have no disagreement. However, no one can convince me he was weak or cowardly in the face of his chronic illness.

The cause of the composer's chronic cough, that idiomatic and incessant interruption that would become so noticeable to his many friends, the ceaseless and uncontrollable trait painfully apparent even to those who attended his concerts, may forever elude our complete understanding. The cause of the enlargement of his heart may also escape detection. Science may never be able to design a scientific inquiry sufficient to unravel the mystery of his disease. Whatever the cause of his illness, it wreaked terrible havoc on Chopin's life and helped turn a spirited and mirthful child into a melancholic and moody adult. His frequent episodes of hemorrhagic coughing, some of them obviously life-threatening, most certainly would have reminded him of his likely prospects for an early grave. Despite his evident frailty, Chopin somehow must have successfully battled his inexorably fatal disease better than most. In fact, he would later be moved to write "I have outlived so many people younger and stronger than I, that I think I must be immortal." Obviously he wasn't, but his music certainly is.

It's possible that his impressive resolve to continue with his compositional efforts, despite his fear of an early death and a shortened career, was only strengthened by his courageous struggle with his disease. Indeed, the concept of superior strength, whether physical or psychological, being inseparable from a struggle with disability is an ancient one.[137] Chopin's physical weakness might have forced him to devote all his dwindling energies to that main passion in life, his composition. As Paganini may have used his suspected hand deformities to overcome the usual hurdles of technical difficulty and achieve near super-human abilities in playing the violin, Chopin's compensatory response to his own frailties—his passionate drive to compose—may have profoundly influenced the course of his art.

Chopin's obsession for writing music often left room for little else during most of his life, and in his last years his inexorably advancing illness would significantly eat away at even that treasured time. Ultimately, he was forced into increasingly frustrating efforts at musical invention, all hampered by an ever-diminishing capability.

The famous architect and inventor of the geodesic dome, Buckminster Fuller, was unknowingly forced by a physical defect to acquire a proficiency for perceptual analysis he would later use to his advantage. His extreme nearsightedness went unrecognized during his early childhood and, although it must have been awkward and inconvenient for him in many ways, it probably led him to acquire an altered perception of the world. What the young Fuller visualized was a world filled more with large and irregular shapes than with any intricate detail. He always credited this visual deficiency of his youth as being a major contributor to his brilliant success with architectural design.[138] His focus had been shifted by a common physical defect, a flaw that quite fortuitously would lead him to a path of discovery. Chopin's increasingly obsessive immersion into musical composition may have been reinforced in a somewhat similar compensatory way by his inexorable physical decline. The path to genius is indeed an indiscriminate one.

Above all, Frédéric Chopin will be remembered for his marvelously expressive music and for the impeccable way he was able to render the piano capable of projecting a quality of tone previously unknown. The unparalleled immediacy of his compositions whose emotional content can connect so quickly with listeners has served to endear his works to millions and will undoubtedly similarly continue to excite and soothe generations yet to be born. That his illness had a hand in their melancholic style cannot be doubted. Today, the identity of that mysterious disease provides scientists an intriguing enigma those in future generations may someday solve. One can hope for continued scientific progress in a more enlightened world, a future where the curious can pursue such questions with vigor and passion, unfettered by the restraints of ignorance and dogma. It is essential, however, that an important caveat be kept in mind for future investigations into the identity of Chopin's illness: any penetrating focus on Frédéric Chopin's mortality must not blur the immortality of his musical genius.

Among the many lengthy obituaries written for Chopin, one of my favorites was written by the great Polish poet Cyprian Norwid. Norwid once met Chopin in 1849, not long before the composer's death. That meeting made a profound impression on the young poet, and he would later write a glowing tribute to this musical genius. Interestingly, the lives of Norwid and Chopin shared some common features. They were both autodidacts in their respective fields. They each became Romantic poets with deeply classical roots. They were both born in small villages near Warsaw and never lost their intense love for their home country, no matter where they lived. And, most unfortunately, they both probably suffered and died from the same dreadful disease. Norwid's words describe his friend:

He knew how to divine the greatest mysteries of art with astonishing ease—he could gather the flowers of the field without disturbing the dew or the lightest pollen. And then he knew how to fashion them into stars, meteors, as it were comets, lighting up the sky of Europe, through the ideal of art. In the crystal of his own harmony he gathered the tears of the Polish people strewn over the fields, and placed them as the diamond of beauty in the diadem of humanity. [139]

For now, Chopin's revered heart remains inviolate in its darkened crypt, preserved for the ages, its shadowed score merely the fragment of an unwritten improvisation untiringly waiting behind the curtain for its final encore.

Chopin's tomb in the Père Lachaise Cemetery.

Appendix

A Brief Chronicle of Chopin's Life and Health

Year	Age	Life Events	Health Issues
1810		Chopin born March 1 at Żelazowa Wola; later that year his family moves to Warsaw.	His birth and early childhood are unremarkable for significant health problems.
1816	6	Begins piano lessons with his mother.	
1817	7	Wojciech Żywny becomes his piano instructor; the *Polonaise in G minor* is published.	

Year	Age	Life Events	Health Issues
1818	8	Performs at a charity concert in the Saxon Palace; presents two polonaises (both now lost) to the Empress, Maria Feodorovna.	A childhood friend, Eustachy Marylski, later would describe the young Chopin "as something of a weakling."
1820	10	Performs for the Grand Duke Constantin; receives a gold watch from the famous singer A. Catalani.	Unconfirmed reports of digestive difficulties, possible allergies, and asthma-like respiratory problems.
1822	12	Begins composition lessons with Jósef Elsner.	
1823	13	Enrolls at the Warsaw Lyceum; begins studies in harmony.	A close childhood friend, Jan Białobłocki, is diagnosed with a chronic tubercular infection.
1824	14	Wins first-year prize at the Lyceum; spends summer with friends near Żelazowa Wola.	Parents concerned about his failure to put on weight and his pallor; Dr. Roemer, their family physician, prescribes a special diet along with unspecified "pills."
1825	15	Performs for Tsar Alexander I, who gives him a diamond ring; *Rondo Op. 1* published.	His letters describe an active social life and frequent late-night parties; parents concerned he is neglecting his health.

Year	Age	Life Events	Health Issues
1826	16	Composes *B flat minor Polonaise*; gives several benefit concerts; enters Warsaw Conservatory that fall.	Ill many months with neck lymph node swelling, fatigue, and poor appetite; younger sister, Emilia, also ill; parents send both that summer to Reinertz health spa where Chopin at least partially recovers.
1827	17	Composes *Là ci darem Variations* and *C minor Sonata*.	Emilia dies suddenly of a massive hemorrhage at the age of 14; close friend Jan Białobłocki dies after a long battle with tuberculosis.
1828	18	Visits Berlin; composes *Rondo à la Krokowiak, Op. 14.*	Illness prompts stay at health spa at Sanniki; later a Polish physician, Czesław Sielużycki, reported Chopin suffered from "gastric troubles, severe headaches, and rotting teeth" during this time.
1829	19	Hears Paganini perform in Warsaw; meets Hummel; graduates from the Conservatory; travels to Vienna where he gives two successful concerts.	

Year	Age	Life Events	Health Issues
1830	20	Performs his two concertos at public concerts in Warsaw; leaves Poland and travels to Vienna.	An unsubstantiated report claims that he suffers from a recurrence of the illness that plagued him in 1826.
1831	21	Spends many tedious and unsuccessful months in Vienna; performs in Munich and later in Stuttgart; in October arrives in Paris where he meets Liszt and Hiller.	Narrowly avoids Vienna cholera epidemic; suffers depressive illness after multiple frustrations; later has an emotional collapse in Stuttgart when he learns of the failure of the Polish Uprising against Russia.
1832	22	First public concert in Paris a big success; enjoys friendships with Liszt, Berlioz, Mendelssohn; begins lucrative teaching career.	Some reports of his frail appearance and pallor.
1833	23	Performs at a benefit concert with Liszt; friendship with Bellini; adds several new pupils to his growing list of students; *Op. 10 Études* published.	

Year	Age	Life Events	Health Issues
1835	25	Enjoys reunion with parents at Carlsbad; falls in love with Maria Wodzińska; visits Leipzig where he meets Mendelssohn, Clara Wieck, and Schumann.	Maria's parents concerned about his health; falls seriously ill with bronchitis that fall; reports of his death circulate in Warsaw; frightened, he writes his will.
1836	26	Proposes to Maria at Marienbad. Her parents insist on indefinite delay of their marriage; in October meets George Sand at party in Paris.	Suffers another bout of respiratory illness during the winter; weakness and debility worsen.
1837	27	Maria's parents end her engagement; growing friendship with Sand; *Op. 25, Opp. 29-32* published.	Winter respiratory problems with coughing and bronchial bleeding.
1838	28	Liaison with Sand begins; travels to Majorca with Sand and her children; completes the *Préludes, Op. 28.*	Suffers severe respiratory collapse with major bronchial hemorrhaging while at Valldemossa that winter.

Year	Age	Life Events	Health Issues
1839	29	After a disastrous winter, leaves Majorca to spend the summer recuperating at Sand's ancestral home in Nohant; completes the *B minor Sonata, Op. 35.*	Diagnosed with "consumption" by physicians in Valldemossa, he is forced to leave; receives emergent treatment for hemorrhaging in Marseilles; recovers in Nohant.
1840	30	In Paris the entire year, teaching and composing; *Opp. 35-42* published.	Chronically ill and increasingly frail, he suffers from an incessant cough and frequent fevers.
1841	31	Second public concert in Paris; spends another summer in Nohant; *Opp. 43-49* published.	Friends express alarm at the state of his health; further weight loss.
1842	32	Performs concert with cellist Auguste Franchomme and singer Pauline Viardot; friendship with painter Eugène Delacroix grows; *Op. 50* published.	Shocked and saddened by death of close friend, Jan Matuszyński (from tuberculosis); continued respiratory compromise.
1843	33	Publishes *Ballade in F minor, Op. 52, the Polonaise in A flat major, Op. 53,* and the *Scherzo in E major.*	Weakness forces him to withdraw from further public performances.

Year	Age	Life Events	Health Issues
1844	34	Chopin's father dies from suspected tuberculosis; older sister, Ludwika, visits him in Nohant; publishes *Nocturnes, Op. 55* and *Three Mazurkas, Op. 56.*	Chronic illness aggravates his struggle with composition; in letter to Sand (December 2) writes, "Always yours, older than ever; very, extremely, incredibly old…"
1845	35	Relationship with Sand deteriorates; publishes *Three Mazurkas, Op. 59, Barcarolle, Op. 60.*	Dramatic worsening of overall health; notes difficulties with memory.
1846	36	Sand publishes her novel, *Lucrezia Floriani,* a thinly veiled unflattering caricature of Chopin; publishes the *Polonaise-fantasie, Op. 61.*	Relationship with Sand strained by his near-invalid status; chronic cough and shortness of breath worsen.
1847	37	Breaks with Sand after disagreement over her daughter Solange's marriage to the sculptor, Auguste Clésinger; financial worries mount; *Sonata for Piano and Cello, Op. 65* published.	Unable to teach due to poor health; remains largely housebound; receives homeopathic care from Dr. Molin.

Year	Age	Life Events	Health Issues
1848	38	His pupil Jane Stirling begins an unreciprocated romantic interest; gives final concert in Paris just prior to 1848 Revolution; travels with Stirling to England and Scotland where he gives public concerts in Manchester, Glasgow, and London.	Needs to be carried and dressed; declining health shortens trip to England and Scotland and forces return to Paris.
1849	39	Assisted financially by Stirling and friends; Ludwika summoned and arrives to nurse him through final illness; dies in Paris on October 17.	Alarmed by abdominal and leg swelling, consults Drs. Cruveilhier, Blache, and Louis in desperate attempt at cure; dies of progressive respiratory failure; Cruveilhier removes Chopin's heart and preserves it in alcohol solution, October 20; funeral at the Madeleine in Paris, October 30.

Illustrations

Portrait of Chopin by T. Kwiatkowski. This remarkable painting was long held by Alfred Cortot, one of the supreme interpreters of Chopin's music. Although he mistakenly attributed the work to a M. Rubio, Cortot believed after years of careful study that this painting most truly captured the essence of Chopin's features. Painting by Thèophile Kwiatkowski, *Collection: Fryderyk Chopin Museum;* Courtesy of *The Fryderyk Chopin Institute,* Warsaw.

The repository for Chopin's preserved heart in the Holy Cross Church in Warsaw. The inscription reads, "For Where Your Treasure Is, There Your Heart Will Be." The relic was temporarily removed during the 1944 Warsaw Uprising of WWII and reinterred in 1951. (Photograph by the author.)

The penciled deathbed note long attributed to Chopin, "If this cough should suffocate me, I beseech you to have my body opened that I'll not be buried alive." Recent research now asserts that it was written in 1844 by Chopin's father during his own protracted death struggle. Ekiert, Janusz, *Fryderyk Chopin, An Illustrated Biography,* (MUZA SA, Warsaw 2009, 2010), p. 61.

Nohant, the ancestral home of George Sand, where she and Chopin spent many idyllic summers, often joined by the painter Eugène Delacroix, as well as several other close friends. (Photograph by the author.)

Nohant, the rear view. The second-floor window was Chopin's room, where he composed at the piano. Guests would often seat themselves just below the window to hear the most glorious music on warm summer nights. (Photograph by the author.)

The gardens of Nohant. (Photograph by the author.)

Żelazowa Wola, Chopin's birthplace in Poland. Although he lived here only six months before his family moved to Warsaw, he frequently returned for visits during his youth. *Collection: Fryderyk Chopin Museum;* Courtesy of *The Fryderyk Chopin Institute,* Warsaw.

Chopin's parents, Justyna and Nicholas, (Mikołaj). She had been Justyna Krzyżanowska. He was born French yet claimed Polish ancestry. Drawing by Ambroży Mieroszewski. *Collection: Fryderyk Chopin Museum*; Courtesy of *The Fryderyk Chopin Institute,* Warsaw.

Adalbert Żywny (1756-1842). Chopin's first piano instructor. Reportedly, he never bathed, preferring occasional vodka sponge baths. Despite his bumpkin ways, he proved to a capable teacher for the young Chopin. Painting by Mieroszewski, (original lost in 1939); *Collection: Fryderyk Chopin Museum;* Courtesy of *The Fryderyk Chopin Institute,* Warsaw.

Emilia Chopin (1812-1827). Chopin's younger sister who died suddenly of a massive bronchial hemorrhage. Miniature on ivory by unknown artist. *Collection: Fryderyk Chopin Museum;* Courtesy of *The Fryderyk Chopin Institute,* Warsaw.

Jósef Elsner (1769-1854). Chopin's second (and last) piano instructor. Lithograph by Maximilian Fajans, Warsaw, 1851, *Collection: Fryderyk Chopin Museum;* Courtesy of *The Fryderyk Chopin Institute,* Warsaw.

Program of Chopin's debut performance in Paris at the original Salle Pleyel. The concert was advertised for January 15, but postponed until February 26, 1832. Six pianists performed at one time, among them, Felix Mendelssohn, Ferdinand Hiller, and Chopin. Orga, Ates, *The Illustrated Lives of the Great Composers: Chopin,* p. 67.

Maria Wodzińska (1819-1896). Penciled self-portrait by Maria Wodzińska at age seventeen (original lost in 1939). *Collection: Fryderyk Chopin Museum;* Courtesy of *The Fryderyk Chopin Institute,* Warsaw.

Portrait of Chopin by Maria Wodzińska. After Chopin proposed to her in 1836, Maria painted this watercolor of her young beau. Her parents eventually refused to sanction their marriage. Maria Wodzińska, watercolor, *Collection: Fryderyk Chopin Museum;* Courtesy of *The Fryderyk Chopin Institute,* Warsaw.

Chopin's packet of letters from Maria Wodzińska. He saved them all his life and marked them, "Moja bieda" ("My trouble"). *Collection: Fryderyk Chopin Museum*; Courtesy of *The Fryderyk Chopin Institute,* Warsaw.

Aurore Dupin Dudevant, aka George Sand, in her male attire. This must have been how she looked when she and Chopin first met. Siepmann, Jeremy, *Chopin, The Reluctant Romantic*, pp. 64-65. (Mary Evans Picture Library.)

An early photograph of George Sand. At 5' 1," she was a small woman with large dark eyes. Zamoyski, Adam, *Chopin, A Biography*, pp. 176-177. (Mansell Collection.)

Painting of George Sand, French novelist and Chopin's companion of nine years. The portrait appears quite stylized and "doctored." *Ibid.* (Mansell Collection.)

Karl Filtch. Of all of Chopin's many students, young Karl was considered the best. Chopin often joked he would stop performing once Filtch began his career. Unfortunately, the boy would succumb to tuberculosis at the age of fifteen. Lithograph by Menut-Alophe, 1843. Eigeldinger, Jean-Jacques, *Chopin: Pianist and Teacher*, p. 141.

Chopin at the piano. Pencil drawing by J. Göetzenberger, Paris, October 1838. Orga, Ates, *The Illustrated Lives of the Great Composers: Chopin*, p. 91.

Jane Wilhelmina Stirling (1804-1859). The Scottish woman who came to Chopin's rescue after his breakup with Sand and who carefully preserved many of the composer's personal items for posterity after his death. *Collection: Museum of the University of Jagiełłonskiego,* Kracow; Courtesy of *The Fryderyk Chopin Institute,* Warsaw.

Daguerreotype of Samuel Hahnemann, the founder of homeopathy, alongside the frontispiece of an 1856 edition of his *Exposition of the Medical Doctrine of Homeopathy.* Chopin's use of Dr. Hahnemann's methods probably extended his life. Atwood, William, *The Parisian Worlds of Frédéric Chopin*, p. 347.

Portrait of René-Théophile-Hyacinthe Laennec, the eminent Paris physician who invented the stethoscope in 1816. This primitive instrument was used by Chopin's physicians in their multiple attempts to diagnose his illness. Boutaric, Jean-José, *Laennec, Balzac, Chopin et le stéthoscope*, p. 14.

Early stethoscopes. The three on the left are like those used on Balzac and Chopin. Courtesy of the Musée d'Histoire de la médecine, Paris. (Photograph by the author.)

The design for an early stethoscope. *Jean-José, Laennec, Balzac, Chopin et le stethoscope,* p. 59.

Honoré de Balzac, the famous French author. Balzac's physicians, making use of the newly invented stethoscope, correctly diagnosed his valvular heart disease years before he died of heart failure. *Collection: Fryderyk Chopin Museum,* Courtesy of *The Fryderyk Chopin Institute,* Warsaw.

Laennec practicing auscultation at the Necker Hospital in Paris. Interestingly, with this patient he appears to prefer using his ear rather than the crude device he holds in his left hand. Taken from a fresco in the Hall of Honor at the Sorbonne in Paris. Boutaric, Jean-José, *Laennec, Balzac, Chopin et le stéthoscope,* p. 212.

Chopin's last apartment at 12, Place Vendôme in Paris. Surrounded by his closest friends, the composer died here on October 17, 1849 (original lost). *Collection: Fryderyk Chopin Museum;* Courtesy of *The Fryderyk Chopin Institute, Warsaw.*

Painting by T. Kwiatkowski, *The Last Moments of Frédéric Chopin.* Chopin's sister, Ludwika, is seated to the left of the composer. *Collection: Fryderyk Chopin Museum;* Courtesy of *The Fryderyk Chopin Institute,* Warsaw.

Chopin on his deathbed just hours after his death. Watercolor/drawing by T. Kwiatkowski, signed October 17, 1849; *Collection: Fryderyk Chopin Museum;* Courtesy of *The Fryderyk Chopin Institute,* Warsaw.

The return of Chopin's heart to Warsaw, 1951. Still taken from a Polish newsreel of the same year. Courtesy of the *Bibliotèque Polonaise,* Paris.

Holy Cross Church, Warsaw Poland. (Photograph by the author.)

Portrait of Jean Baptiste Cruveilhier. Distinguished anatomist and physician, he was Chopin's last physician. His rambling comments on the postmortem findings he encountered as he removed the composer's heart have helped fuel the heated controversy over what caused Chopin's death. Atwood, William, *The Parisian Worlds of Frédéric Chopin,* p. 331.

The plaster cast of Chopin's hand taken after his death by Clésinger. On display at the Bibliothèque Polonaise, Paris. (Photograph by the author.)

The Church of the Madeleine in Paris, completed in 1846. Chopin's funeral was held here in late October 1849. Large black fabric panels were draped across the columns to mark the event. Accounts estimate 4,000 people waited outside for the long procession to the cemetery.

Collection: Fryderyk Chopin Museum; Courtesy of *The Fryderyk Chopin Institute,* Warsaw.

Example of finger clubbing. *Wikipedia.*

Frédéric Chopin (1810-1849). Once considered to have been taken only months prior to Chopin's death in 1849, this daguerreotype by Louis-Auguste Bisson has recently been traced to the latter part of 1847. Assuming it dated from 1849, some medical investigators believed it revealed facial swelling, in their view a possible indicator of end-stage heart disease. *Collection: Fryderyk Chopin Museum;* Courtesy of *the Fryderyk Chopin Institute,* Warsaw. (Recent research done by Malgorzata Maria Grabczewska, *Revue de la Bibliotèque Nationale de France, no. 34, 2010.*)

Niccòlo Paganini (1782-1840). The Italian virtuoso whose extraordinary performances greatly impressed the young Chopin and led the young Pole to write equivalently impressive works for the keyboard. Paganini was forced to retire from the concert stage for health reasons. Many believe he suffered from Marfan's Syndrome. Lithograph by M. Gauci. *Collection: Fryderyk Chopin Museum;* Courtesy of *TheFryderyk Chopin Institute,* Warsaw.

The signature of Frédéric Chopin. *Collection: Fryderyk Chopin Museum;* Courtesy of *The Fryderyk Chopin Institute,* Warsaw.

Lock of Chopin's hair collected after his death by his older sister Ludwika. Might DNA testing of this sample lead to a conclusive answer? *Collection: Fryderyk Chopin Museum;* Courtesy of *The Fryderyk Chopin Institute,* Warsaw.

Chopin's tomb at Père Lachaise in Paris. (Photograph by the author.)

Notes

1. Kubba, A. K., Young, M. 1998. The long suffering of Frédéric Chopin. *Chest* 113:210-216.
2. Majka, L., Gozdzik, J., Witt, M. 2003. Cystic fibrosis—a probable cause of Frédéric Chopin's suffering and death. *J. Appl. Genet.* 44(1):77-84.
3. O'Shea, J. 1987. Was Frédéric Chopin's illness actually cystic fibrosis? *The Medical Journal of Australia,* Vol. 147.
4. Roth, D. September 2008. Chopin, a missing autopsy report, and molecular pathology. *NYU Department of Pathology, Resources.*
5. Mullan, F. 1973. The sickness of Frédéric Chopin. A study of disease and society. *Rocky Mountain Medical Journal* 70:29-34.
6. Samson, J. 1985. *The music of Chopin.* London. Repr. Oxford: Clarendon Press, 1994.
7. Gewert, J. Executive Director, The Chopin Foundation of The United States. 1440 79th Street Causeway, Suite 117, Miami, Florida 33141.
8. International Federation of Chopin Societies. Warsaw, Poland.
9. Szulc, T. 1988. *Chopin in Paris.* Da Capo Press, p. 163.
10. Cichy, W., PhD, MD, Professor of Pediatrics, University of Medical Sciences, Poznan. Founder of Polish Cystic Fibrosis Group of Pediatric Society, 1992; Cofounder of European Cystic Fibrosis Society.
11. Boutaric, J. 2004. *Laennec, Balzac, Chopin et le stethoscope.* Paris: Glyphe & Biotem editions, p. 267.
12. Martin, R. 2000. *Beethoven's hair.* Random House.
13. Liszt, F. 1863. *Life of Chopin.* Oliver Ditson & Co., Boston. Repr. Mineola, New York, Dover Publications, Inc. 2003.
14. Huneker, J. 1966. *Chopin, the man and his music.* New York: Dover Publications, Inc., p. 3.

15. Lawler, C. 2007. *Consumption and Literature.* Basingstoke: Palgrave Macmillan.

16. Browning, E. B. 1862. *Last poems, De profundis.* London.

17. Sand, G. 1902-1904. *Histoire de Ma Vie* (4 vols.) Paris. Trans. D. Hofstader. New York: Harper & Row, 1979.

18. Samson, J. 1996. *Master musicians: Chopin.* Oxford: Oxford University Press, p. 145.

19. Opieński, H. 1988. *Frédéric Chopin: Chopin's letters.* Repr. New York: Dover Publications, Inc., p. 186.

20. Ibid., p. 420.

21. Kubba, A. K., Young, M. 1998. The long suffering of Frédéric Chopin. *Chest,* 113:79.

22. O'Shea, J. 1987. Was Frédéric Chopin's illness actually cystic fibrosis? *The Medical Journal of Australia,* Vol. 147.

23. Ibid., p. 586.

24. Szulc, T. 1988. *Chopin in Paris.* Da Capo Press, p. 100.

25. Davila, J. 1995. Étude De La Maladie De Chopin À Traverse Sa Correspondance, *Université Paul-Sabatier – Toulouse III, Faculty De Medicine, 95 – Tou 3 –* 1084:24; Bibliotèque Polonaise, Paris.

25. Kubba, A. K., Young, M. 1998. The long suffering of Frédéric Chopin. *Chest* 113:210-216.

26. Opieński, H. 1988. *Frédéric Chopin: Chopin's letters.* Repr. New York: Dover Publications, Inc., p. 21.

27. Ibid., p. 28.

28. For the purposes of this book, *Frédéric Chopin* will be the preferred spelling of the Polish original, *Fryderyk Chopin.*

29. Szulc, T. 1988. *Chopin in Paris.* Da Capo Press, p. 38.

30. Zamoyski, A. 1979. *Chopin: A biography.* London: William Collins Sons & Co. Ltd., p. 17.

31. Siepmann, J. 1995. *Chopin, the reluctant romantic.* Boston: Northeastern University Press, p. 24.

32. Zamoyski, A. 1979. *Chopin: A biography.* London: William Collins Sons & Co. Ltd., p. 173.

33. Samson, J. 1996. *Master musicians: Chopin.* Oxford: Oxford University Press, p. 16.

34. Siepmann, J. 1995. *Chopin, the reluctant romantic.* Boston: Northeastern University Press, p. 27.

35. Opieński, H. 1988. *Frédéric Chopin: Chopin's letters.* Repr. New York: Dover Publications, Inc., p. 21.

36. Kumar, V, Abbas, A., Fausto, N., Mitchell, R. 2007. *Robbins basic pathology (*8th edition), Saunders Elsevier, pp. 403-406.

37. Medline Plus Medical Encyclopedia: 2010, *Rheumatic Fever.*

38. Samson, J. 1996. *Master musicians: Chopin.* Oxford: Oxford University Press, p. 23.

39. Szulc, T. 1988. *Chopin in Paris.* Da Capo Press, p. 39.

40. Davila, J. 1995. Étude De La Maladie De Chopin À Traverse Sa Correspondance, *Université Paul-Sabatier – Toulouse III, Faculty De Medicine, 95 – Tou 3* –1084:9; Bibliotèque Polonaise, Paris.

40. Szulc, T. 1988. *Chopin in Paris.,* Da Capo Press, p. 40.

41. Opieński, H. 1988. *Frédéric Chopin: Chopin's letters.* Repr. New York: Dover Publications, Inc., p. 56.

42. Ibid., p. 132.

43. Ibid., p. 148-150.

44. Cortot, A. 1975. *In Search of Chopin.* Repr. Westport, Connecticut: Greenwood Press, Publishers, p. 114.

45. Siepmann, J. 1995. *Chopin, the reluctant romantic.* Boston: Northeastern University Press, p. 86.

46. Opieński, H. 1988. *Frédéric Chopin: Chopin's letters.* Repr. New York: Dover Publications, Inc., p. 175.

47. Davila, J. 1995. Étude De La Maladie De Chopin À Traverse Sa Correspondance, *Université Paul-Sabatier – Toulouse III, Faculty De Medicine, 95 – Tou 3* – 1084:35; Bibliotèque Polonaise, Paris.

48. Siepmann, J. 1995. *Chopin, the reluctant romantic.* Boston: Northeastern University Press, p. 123.

49. Ibid., p. 124.

50. Siepmann, J. 1995. *Chopin, the reluctant romantic.* Boston: Northeastern University Press, 131.

51. Cawthorne, N. 1998. *Sex Lives of the Great Composers.* London: Prion, p. 73.

52. Szulc, T. 1988. *Chopin in Paris.* Da Capo Press, p. 207.

53. Davila, J. 1995. Étude De La Maladie De Chopin À Traverse Sa Correspondance, *Université Paul-Sabatier – Toulouse III, Faculty De Medicine, 95 – Tou 3* – 1084:55; Bibliotèque Polonaise, Paris.

54. Sand, G. 1993. *Un Hiver à Majorque.* Paris: Editions Glénat.

55. Kubba, A. K., Young, M. 1998. The long suffering of Frédéric Chopin. *Chest* 113:216.

56. Opieński, H. 1988. *Frédéric Chopin: Chopin's letters.* Repr. New York: Dover Publications, Inc., p. 192.

57. Cortot, A. 1949. *Aspects de Chopin.* Paris: Editions Albin Michel, p. 121.

58. Liszt, F. 1863. *Life of Chopin.* Oliver Ditson & Co., Boston. Repr. Mineola, New York, Dover Publications, Inc. 2003.

59. Gibbs, C. H. 2000. *The life of Schubert.* Cambridge University Press.

60. Szulc, T. 1988. *Chopin in Paris.* Da Capo Press, p. 344.

61. Howarth, T. 1962. *Citizen king: The life of Louis-Philippe, king of the French.* Eyre & Spottiswoode.

62. Meissner, M. 1992. Samuel Hahnemann—the originator of homeopathic medicine. *Krakenpflege Journal* 30(7-8):364-366.

63. Davila, J. 1995. Étude De La Maladie De Chopin À Traverse Sa Correspondance, *Université Paul-Sabatier – Toulouse III, Faculty De Medicine, 95 – Tou 3 – 1084*:79-82; Bibliotèque Polonaise, Paris.

64. Ibid., p. 92.

65. Ibid., p. 92.

66. Opieński, H. 1988. *Frédéric Chopin: Chopin's letters.* Repr. New York: Dover Publications, Inc., p. 387.

67. Ibid., p. 397.

68. Szulc, T. 1988. *Chopin in Paris.* Da Capo Press, p. 391.

69. Majka, L., Gozdzik, J., Witt, M. 2003. Cystic fibrosis—a probable cause of Frédéric Chopin's suffering and death. *J. Appl. Genet.* 44(1):77-84.

70. Boutaric, J. 2004. *Laennec, Balzac, Chopin et le stethoscope.* Paris: Glyphe & Biotem editions, p. 53.

71. Ibid., p. 239.

72. Szulc, T. 1988. *Chopin in Paris.* Da Capo Press, p. 396.

73. Zamoyski, A. 1979. *Chopin: A biography.* London: William Collins Sons & Co. Ltd., p. 282.

74. Ekiert, J. 2009-2010. *Fryderyk Chopin, an illustrated biography.* MUZA SA, Warsaw, p. 61.

75. Heldey, A. 1962. *Selected correspondence of Chopin.* London: Heinemann, pp. 73-74.

76. Davila, J. 1995. Étude De La Maladie De Chopin À Traverse Sa Correspondance, *Université Paul-Sabatier – Toulouse III, Faculty De Medicine, 95 – Tou 3 – 1084*:106; Bibliotèque Polonaise, Paris.

77. Hoesick, F. U. October, 1899. *Country, No. 41 (20),* p. 201.

78. Biełoszewski, M. 1984. *Memoir of the Warsaw Uprising.* Warsaw, p. 127.

79. Tebinka, J. 2002. *Ciche lata kata Polityka, nr* (32)2362:66.

80. Kakolewski, K. 1973. Generale Reinefarth, do you know your nickname? *Literature No. 22:1, 3.*

81. Sydow, B. E. 1945. The heart of Frederic Chopin, *Traffic Music 3:2-4.*

82. Gilljam, M., Ellis, M., Corey, J., et. al. 2004. Clinical manifestations of cystic fibrosis among patients with diagnosis in adulthood. *Chest* 126:1215-1224.

83. Drumm, M. L., Konstan, M. D., Schlucter, A., et. al. 2005. Genetic modifiers of lung disease in cystic fibrosis. *New England Journal of Medicine* 353:1443-1453.

84. Farrell, Phillip, et. al. August 2008. Guidelines for diagnosis of cystic fibrosis in newborns through older adults: Cystic fibrosis consensus report. *The Journal of Pediatrics* 153(2):S4-S14.

85. Chmiel, J. F., Drum, M. W., Konstan, T.W., et. al. 1999. Pitfalls in the use of genotype analysis as the sole diagnostic criterion for cystic fibrosis. *Pediatrics* 103:823-826.

86. Kallmann, F. J., Reisner, D. 1943. Twin studies on the significance of genetic factors in tuberculosis. *Am. Rev. Tuberc.* 16:593-617.

87. Delhoume, L. 1937. *L'Ecole de Dupuytren—Jean Cruveilhier.* Paris.

88. Boutaric, J. 2004. *Laennec, Balzac, Chopin et le stethoscope.* Paris: Glyphe & Biotem editions, pp. 281-325.

89. Kubba, A. K., Young, M. 1998. The long suffering of Frédéric Chopin. *Chest* 113:215.

90. Ibid., p. 214.

91. Axelsson, U., Laurell, C. B., 1965. Hereditary variants of serum alpha 1-antitrypsin. *Am. J. Genet.* 17(6):466-472.

92. Ferra, R. C., Valldemossa, M. 2008. Personal correspondence regarding family trees of Frédéric Chopin and George Sand.

93. Kubba, A. K., Young, M. 1998. The long suffering of Frédéric Chopin. *Chest* 113:215.

94. DeMaine MD, J. Pulmonologist. Personal communication.

95. Szulc, T. 1988. *Chopin in Paris.* Da Capo Press, p. 410.

96. Cortot, A. 1949. *Aspects de Chopin; La Main De Chopin.* Paris: Editions Albin Michel, p. 26.

97. "Poland says Chopin's heart won't undergo DNA testing," *The Seattle Times,* July 26, 2008.

98. Majka, L., Gozdzik, J., Witt, M. 2003. Cystic fibrosis—a probable cause of Frédéric Chopin's suffering and death. *J. Appl. Genet.* 44(1):82.

99. Ibid., p. 83.

100. Gutierrez, M. C., Brisse, S., Brosch, R., et. al. 2005. Ancient origin and gene mosaicism of the progenitor of Mycobacterium tuberculosis. *PLoS Pathog.* 1(1):e5.doi10.137/journal. ppat.0010005).

101. *Fact Sheet: Tuberculosis in the United States.* Center for Disease Control. March 17, 2005. Retrieved October, 2006.

102. "Stop partnership, London tuberculosis rates now at third world proportions," *PR Newswire LTD.* December 4, 2002.

103. *Tuberculosis Fact Sheet No. 104, Global and regional incidence.* World Health Organization. March 2006.

104. Ibid.

105. Nnoaham, K., Clarke, A. 2008. Low serum vitamin D levels and tuberculosis: A systematic review and meta-analysis. *Int. J. Epidemiol.* 37:113-119.

106. Ustianowski, A., Shaffer, R., Collin, S., et. al. June 2005. Prevalence and associations of vitamin D deficiency in foreign-born persons with tuberculosis in London. *The Journal of Infection* 50(5):432-7.

107. Anders, J. 1909. The incidence and causes of hemoptysis—a statistical study. *Transactions of the American Clinical and Climatological Association, Trans. Am. Climatolog. Assoc.* 25:27-36.

108. Ibid.

109. Kallmann, F. J., Reisner, D. 1943. Twin studies on the significance of genetic factors in tuberculosis. J. Hered. 34 (9): 269-276.

110. Majka, L., Gozdzik, J., Witt, M. 2003. Cystic fibrosis—a probable cause of Frédéric Chopin's suffering and death. *J. Appl. Genet.* 44(1):77-84.

111. Wiuf, C. August 2001. Do delta F508 heterozygotes have a selective advantage? *Genet. Res.* 78(1):41-47.

112. Modiano, G., et. al. March 2007. Cystic fibrosis and lactase persistence: a possible correlation. *Eur. J. Hum. Genet.* 15(3):255-9.

113. "Ottawa University boots cystic fibrosis from charity drive," *National Post*, November 25, 2008.

114. O'Shea, J. 1987. Was Frédéric Chopin's illness actually cystic fibrosis? *The Medical Journal of Australia* 147:586.

115. Majka, L., Gozdzik, J., Witt, M. 2003. Cystic fibrosis—a probable cause of Frédéric Chopin's suffering and death. *(J. Appl. Genet.* 44(1), 2003, p. 78.

116. Farrell, P., et. al. August 2008. Guidelines for diagnosis of cystic fibrosis in newborns through older adults: Cystic fibrosis consensus report. *The Journal of Pediatrics* 153(2):S4-S14.

117. Augarten, A., Yahav, Y., Kerem, B., Halle, D., et. al. 1994. Congenital bilateral absence of vas deferens of cystic fibrosis. *Lancet* 344:1473-1474.

118. Marks, S. C., Kissner, D. G., January-February 1997. Management of sinusitis in adult cystic fibrosis. *Am. J. Rhinol.* 11(1):11-4.

119. DeMaine MD, J. Pulmonologist. Personal communication.

120. Myocardial tuberculosis. 2008. *Nat. Clin. Pract. Cardiovasc. Med.* 5(3):169-174.

121. Boutaric, J. 2004. *Laennec, Balzac, Chopin et le stethoscope.* Paris: Glyphe & Biotem editions, p. 385.

122. Chmiel, J. F., Drum, M. W., Konstan, T. W., et. al. 1999. Pitfalls in the use of genotype analysis as the sole diagnostic criterion for cystic fibrosis. *Pediatrics* 103:823-826.

123. Majka, L., Pogorzelski, A., Mlynarczk, W., et. al., 2001. Effect of genotype on selected clinical features of Polish cystic fibrosis adults. *J. Appl. Genet.* 42(3):367-377.

124. Schoenfeld, M. R. January 2, 1978. Niccòlo Paganini: Musical magician and Marfan mutant? *JAMA* 239(1).

125. Starr, F. 2000. *Louis Moreau Gottshalk.* University of Illinois Press.

126. The death of Louis Moreau Gottshalk was probably a fatal heart rhythm induced by an inadvertent overdose of quinine he had been using for his malarial symptoms.

127. Barnes, J. 2008. *Nothing to be frightened of.* London: Jonathan Cape, p. 205.

128. Thomas, D. 1952. Do not go gentle into that good night, *The Poems of Dylan Thomas.* New Directions.

129. Massie, R. F. 1995. *The Romanovs: The final chapter.* Random House, pp. 194-229.

130. Coble, M., et. al. 2009. Mystery solved: The identification of the two missing Romanov children using DNA analysis. *Plos One* 4(3): e4838.doi:10.131/journal.pone.0004838.

131. Filon, D., Faerman, M., Smith P., Oppenheim A. 1995. Sequence analysis reveals a beta-thalassemia mutation in the DNA of skeletal remains from the archeological site of Akhziv, Israel. *Nature Genetics* 9:365-368.

132. "Recalls look at Lincoln's face in tomb," *Chicago Tribune,* February 4, 1962.

133. Martin, R. 2000. *Beethoven's hair.* Random House.

134. Michalski, G. Director, The Fryderyk Chopin Institute, Warsaw. Personal communication.

135. Armory, S., Keyser, C., Crubezy, E., et. al. 2007. STR typing of ancient DNA extracted from hair of Siberian mummies. *Forensic Science Intl* 166:218-229.

136. Michalski, G. Director, The Fryderyk Chopin Institute, Warsaw. Personal communication.

137. Wilson, E. 1978. *The wound and the bow.* New York: Farrar Straus Giroux, p. 235.

138. Sieden, L. 2000. *Buckminster Fuller's universe, his life and work.* Cambridge, Mass: Perseus Pub.

139. Norwid, C. October 25, 1849. *Dziennik Polski.* Posnan.

Sources

Abbot, C. 1982. Composers and tuberculosis, the effects on creativity. *Journal of the Canadian Medical Association* 126:534-544.

Anders, J. 1909. The incidence and causes of hemoptysis—a statistical study. *Transactions of the American Clinical and Climatological Association* 25:27-36.

Armory, S., Keyser, C., Crubezy, E., et. al. 2007. STR typing of ancient DNA extracted from hair of Siberian mummies. *Forensic Science Intl. 166:218-229.*

Aronson, S. "Chopin died young, but not of tuberculosis," *Scripps News,* 15:57, May 7, 2007.

Atwood, W. 1999. *The Parisian worlds of Frédéric Chopin.* New Haven and London: Yale University Press.

Augarten, A., Yahav, Y., Kerem, B., Halle, D., et. al. 1994. Congenital bilateral absence of vas deferens of cystic fibrosis. *Lancet* 344:1473-74.

Axelsson, U., Laurell, C. B. 1965. Hereditary variants of serum alpha 1-antitrypsin. *Am. J. Genet.* 17(6):466-472.

Barnes, J. 2008. *Nothing to be Frightened of.* London: Jonathan Cape.

Biełoszewski, M. 1984. *Memoir of the Warsaw Uprising, Warsaw,* p. 127.

Bobadilla, J. L., et. al. June 2002. Cystic fibrosis: A worldwide analysis of CFTR mutations—correlation with incidence data and applications to screening. *Human Mutation* 19(6):575-606.

Boutaric, J. 2004. *Laennec, Balzac, Chopin et le stéthoscope.* Paris: Glyphe & Biotem editions.

Browning, E. B. 1862. *Last Poems; De Profundis.* London.

Cate, C. 1975. *George Sand: A biography.* New York: Avon Books.

Cawthorne, N. 1998. *Sex lives of the great composers.* London: Prion.

Centers for Disease Control and Prevention (CDC), Division of Tuberculosis Elimination. 2000. *Core Curriculum on Tuberculosis: What the Clinician Should Know.* 4th ed. Updated August 2003.

Centers for Disease Control. *Fact Sheet: Tuberculosis in the United States* March 17, 2005. Retrieved October. 2006.

Chicago Tribune. February 4, 1962. "Recalls look at Lincoln's face in tomb."

Chmiel, J. F., Drum, M. W., Konstan, T. W., et. al. 1999. Pitfalls in the use of genotype analysis as the sole diagnostic criterion for cystic fibrosis. *Pediatrics* 103:823-826.

Coble, M., et. al. 2009. Mystery solved: The identification of the two missing Romanov children using DNA analysis. *Plos One* 4(3): e4838. doi:10.131/journal.pone.0004838.

Columbo, C., Russo, M. C., Zazzeron, L. Romano, G. July 2006. Liver disease in cystic fibrosis. *Journal of Pediatric Gastroenterology & Nutrition* 43 Suppl 1:S49-55.

Cortot, A. 1949. *Aspects de Chopin.* Paris: Editions Albin Michel.

——. 1975. *In Search of Chopin.* Westport, Connecticut: Greenwood Press, Publishers.

Cruveilhier, J. B. 1829-1842. *Anatomie pathologique du corps humain.* Paris.

Cuthbert, A., Halstead, J., Ratcliff, R., et. al. January 15, 1995. The genetic advantage hypothesis in cystic fibrosis heterozygotes: A murine study. *J. Physiology* 482:449-454.

Cystic Fibrosis Foundation. April 26, 2006. "New statistics show CF patients living longer."

Davila, J. 1996, Étude De La Maladie De Chopin À Traverse Sa Correspondance, *Université Paul-Sabatier—Toulouse III.* Bibliotèque Polonaise, Paris.

Davis, L. 1995. Vegetarian diet and tuberculosis in immigrant Asians. *Thorax* 50(8):915-916.

Dequeker, E, Sturhrmann, M, et. al. January 2009. Best practice guidelines for molecular genetic diagnosis of cystic fibrosis and CFTR-related disorders—updated European recommendations. *Eur J Hum Genet.* 17(1):51-65. Epub August 6, 2008.

Delhoume, L. 1937. *L'Ecole de Dupuytren—Jean Cruveilhier.* Paris.

Dodge, J. A. September 2, 1995. Male fertility in cystic fibrosis. *Lancet* 346(8975):587-588.

Dormandy, T. 2000. *The White Death.* New York: NYU Press.

Drumm, M. L., Konstan, M. D., Schlucter, A., et. al. 2005. Genetic modifiers of lung disease in cystic fibrosis. *New England Journal of Medicine* 353:1443-1453.

Eigeldinger, J. 1986. *Chopin: Pianist and teacher.* Cambridge: Cambridge University Press.

——. 2010. *Chopin et Pleyel.* Librairie Artheme Fayard.

Eisler, B. 2003. *Chopin's funeral.* New York: Alfred A. Knopf.

Ekiert, J. 2009-2010. *Fryderyk Chopin, an illustrated biography.* MUZA SA, Warsaw.

Eriksson, S. July 24, 2003. Did Chopin suffer of antitrypsin deficiency? *Lafartidningen* 100(30-31):2449-2454.

Farrell, P., et. al. August 2008. Guidelines for diagnosis of cystic fibrosis in newborns through older adults: Cystic fibrosis consensus report. *The Journal of Pediatrics* 153(2):S4-S14.

Ferra, R. C. 2008. Valldemossa, Majorca. Personal correspondence. Family trees of Chopin and Sand.

Filon, D., Faerman, M., Smith, P., Oppenheim, A. 1995. Sequence analysis reveals beta-thalassemia mutation in the DNA of skeletal remains from the archeological site of Akhziv, Israel. *Nature Genetics* 9:365-368.

Fryderyk Chopin Institute, Warsaw. 2006. *Plac Piłsudskiego* 9, PL-00-0078. Warsaw, Poland.

Gibbs, C. H. 2000. *The Life of Schubert.* Cambridge University Press.

Gilljam, M., Ellis, M., Corey, J., et. al. 2004. Clinical manifestations of cystic fibrosis among patients with diagnosis in adulthood. *Chest* 126:1215-1224.

Grabczewska, M. M. 2010. Portraits au Daguerréotype de Frederic Chopin. *Revue de la Bibliotèque Nationale de France* 34.

Griffith, D., Kerr, C. 2006. Tuberculosis: Disease of the past, disease of the present. *Journal Perianesth. Nurs.* (4):240-245.

Gutierrez, M. C., Brisse, S., Brosch, R., et. al. 2005. Ancient origin and genemosaicism of the progenitor of Mycobacterium tuberculosis. *PLoS Pathog.* 1(1):e5.doi10.137/journal.ppat.0010005.

Hedley, A. 1947. *Chopin.* London.

——. 1962. *Selected correspondence of Chopin.* London: Heinemann.

Hoesick, F. 1910-1911. *Chopin, his life and work,* 3 vols. Warsaw.

——. *Country,* October, 1899. No. 41, vol. (20), p. 201.

Howarth, T. 1962. *Citizen king: The life of Louis-Philippe, king of the French.* Eyre & Spottiswoode.

Huneker, J. 1966. *Chopin, the man and his music.* New York: Dover Publications, Inc.

Lawler, C. 2007. *Consumption and literature.* Basingstoke: Palgrave Macmillan.

Liszt, F. 1863. *Life of Chopin.* Oliver Ditson & Co., Boston. Repr. Mineola, New York, Dover Publications, Inc. 2003.

Kakolewski, K. 1973. Generale Reinefarth, do you know your nickname? *Literature* 22:1, 3.

Kallberg, J. 1996. *Chopin at the boundaries.* Cambridge, Massachusetts & London, Harvard University Press.

Kallmann, F. J., Reisner, D. 1943. Twin studies on the significance of genetic factors in tuberculosis. J. Hered. 34 (9).

Karasowski, M. 1879. *Life and letters of Chopin.* London: W. Reeves.

Kubba, A. K., Young, M. 1998. The long suffering of Frédéric Chopin. *Chest* 113:210-216.

Kumar, V., Abbas, A., Fausto, N., Mitchell, R. 2007. Robbins basic pathology (8th edition), Saunders Elsevier, 403-406; 516-522.

Kunicki, Ławecki, Olchowik-Adamowska. 2010. *Following Chopin.* Kraków, Colonel.

Kuzemko, J. 1994. Chopin illnesses. *Journal of the Royal Society of Medicine* 87:769-772.

Majka, L., Gozdzik, J., Witt, M. 2003. Cystic fibrosis—a probable cause of Frédéric Chopin's suffering and death. *J. Appl. Genet.* 44(1):77-84.

Majka, L., Pogorzelski, A., Mlynarczk, W., et. al. 2001. Effect of genotype on selected clinical features of Polish cystic fibrosis adults. *J. Appl. Genet.* 42(3):367-377.

Marek, G. 1978. *Chopin.* New York: Harper & Row.

Marks, S. C., Kissner, D. G. January-February 1997. Management of sinusitis in adult cystic fibrosis. *Am. J. Rhinol.* 11(1):11-14.

Martin, R. 2000. *Beethoven's hair.* Random House.

Massie, R. F. 1995. *The Romanovs: The final chapter.* Random House, pp. 194-229.

Medline Plus Medical Encyclopedia: 2010. Rheumatic Fever.

Meissner, M. 1992. Samuel Hahnemann—the originator of homeopathic medicine *Krakenpflege Journal* 30(7-8):364-366.

Modiano, G., et. al. March 2007. Cystic fibrosis and lactase persistence: A possible correlation. *Eur. J. Hum. Genet.* 15(3):255-259.

Mullan, F. 1973. The sickness of Frédéric Chopin. A study of disease and society. *Rocky Mountain Medical Journal*, vol 70: 29-34.

National Institute of Allergy and Infectious Diseases (NIAD). October 2005. "According to the World Heath Organization (WHO), nearly 2 billion people, one-third of the world's population, have TB," (1). Retrieved October 2006.

Nicholas, J. 2007. *Chopin: His life & music*. Naperville, Illinois: Sourcebooks mediaFusion.

Niecks, F. 1887. *The life of Chopin*. London: Faber & Faber.

Nnoaham, K., Clarke, A. 2008. Low serum vitamin D levels and tuberculosis: A systematic review and meta-analysis. *Int. J. Epidemiol.* 37:113-119.

Norwid, C. October 25, 1849. *Dziennik Polski*. Posnan 117.

Ojeda Reyes, F. 2001. *El Desterrado de Paris*. Paris, pp. 20, 29-30.

Opieński, H. 1988. *Frédéric Chopin: Chopin's letters*. Repr. New York: Dover Publications, Inc.

"Ottawa University boots cystic fibrosis from charity drive," *National Post*, November 25, 2008.

Orga, A. 1976. *The illustrated lives of the great composers: Chopin*. London/New York/Sydney/Cologne, Omnibus Press.

O'Shea, J. 1993. Music and medicine. *Journal of Medical Dentistry.*

——. 1987. Was Frédéric Chopin's illness actually cystic fibrosis? *The Medical Journal of Australia* 147.

Persson, H., Wikman, B., Strandvik, B. 2005. Frédéric Chopin—The man, his music, and his illness. *PubMed.gov, US National Library of Medicine, National Institutes of Health, Przegl Lek* 62(6):321-325.

Prochaszka, J. 1969. *Chopin and bohemia*. Prague: Artia.

Ramalho, A. S., Beck, S., Meyer, M., et. al. 2002. Five percent of normal cystic fibrosis transmembrane conductance regulator mRNA ameliorates the severity of pulmonary disease in cystic fibrosis. *Am. J. Respir. Cell. Mol. Biol.* 27(5):619-627.

Rosenstein, B. J., Cutting, G., April, 1998. The diagnosis of cystic fibrosis: a consensus statement (*Cystic Fibrosis Foundation Consensus*) *J. Pediatrics* 132(4):589-595.

Roth, D. September 2008. Chopin, a missing autopsy report, and molecular pathology. *NYU Department of Pathology, Resources.*

Rowe, S. M., Miller, S., Sorscher, 2005. E. J. Cystic Fibrosis. *New England Journal of Medicine* 12:352.

Samson, J. 1996. *Master musicians: Chopin.* Oxford: Oxford University Press.

——. 1992. *The Cambridge Companion to Chopin.* Cambridge, UK: Cambridge University Press.

——. 1985. *The Music of Chopin.* London. Repr. Oxford: Clarendon Press, 1994.

Sand, G. 1902-1904. *Histoire de Ma Vie.* 4 vols. Paris. Translated by D. Hofstader. New York: Harper & Row, 1979.

——. 1993. *Un Hiver à Majorque.* Paris: Editions Glénat.

Schoenfeld, M. R. January 2, 1978. Niccòlo Paganini: Musical magician and Marfan mutant? *JAMA* 239(1).

Sieden, L. 2000. *Buckminster Fuller's universe, his life and work.* Cambridge, Mass., Perseus Pub.

Siepmann, J. 1995. *Chopin, The Reluctant Romantic.* Boston: Northeastern University Press.

Starr, F. 2000. *Louis Moreau Gottshalk.* University of Illinois Press.

"Stop partnership, London tuberculosis rates now at third world proportions," *PR Newswire LTD.,* December 4, 2002. Retrieved October 3, 2006.

Sydow, B. E., The Heart of Frédéric Chopin. *Traffic Music* 3/1945:2-4.

Szulc, T. 1988. *Chopin in Paris.* Da Capo Press.

Tebinka, J. August 10, 2002. Ciche lata kata Polityka, nr 32(2362).

The Seattle Times, "Poland says Chopin's heart won't undergo DNA testing," July 26, 2008.

Thierry, S., Godeau, J. 2010. *Frédéric Chopin, La Note bleue.* Musee de la Vie Romantique, Paris Musees, Paris.

Thomas, D. 1952. Do not go gentle into that good night. *The Poems of Dylan Thomas.* New Directions.

Ustianowski, A., Shaffer, R., Collin, S., et. al. June 2005. Prevalence and associations of vitamin D deficiency in foreign-born persons with tuberculosis in London. *The Journal of Infection* 50(5):432-437.

Von Sternberg, C. 1920. *Tempo Rubato and other essays.* New York and Boston: G. Schirmer.

Wilson, E. 1978. *The wound and the bow.* New York: Farrar Straus Giroux, p. 235.

Wiuf, C. August 2001. Do delta F508 heterozygotes have a selective advantage? *Genet. Res.* 78(1):41-47.

World Health Organization, *Tuberculosis Fact Sheet No. 104, Global and regional incidence*, March 2006.

Zamoyski, A. 1979. *Chopin: A biography.* London: William Collins Sons & Co. Ltd.

Zink, A., Sola, C., Reischl, U., et. al. 2003. Characterization of Mycobacterium tuberculosis complex DNAs from Egyptian mummies by spoligotyping. *J. Clin. Microbiol.* 419(1):359-367.